Usborne

200 Paper Planes to fold & fly

Illustrated by Andy Tudor

Designed by Hannah Ahmed,
Tom Lalonde and Brian Voakes

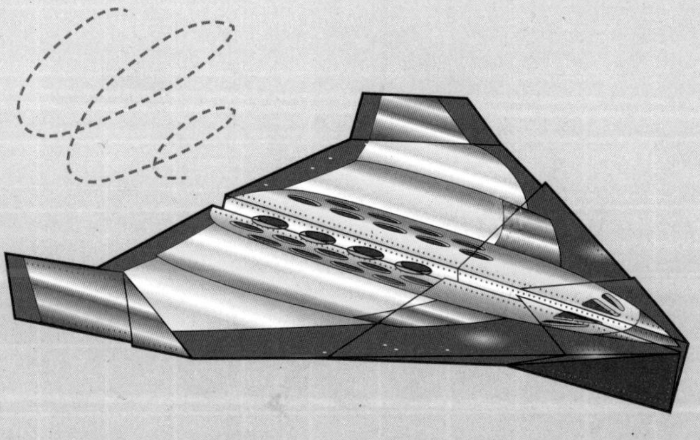

Turn over for tips on flying, folding and looking after your paper planes.

Useful tips

Here are some helpful tips that will make your paper planes fly more effectively and last longer.

How to fly your plane

Here are the best steps to a perfect take-off and landing:

- Stand facing forward.
- Hold your plane just in front of the middle of its body.
- Pull back and then throw forward in a long, smooth movement to release your plane.

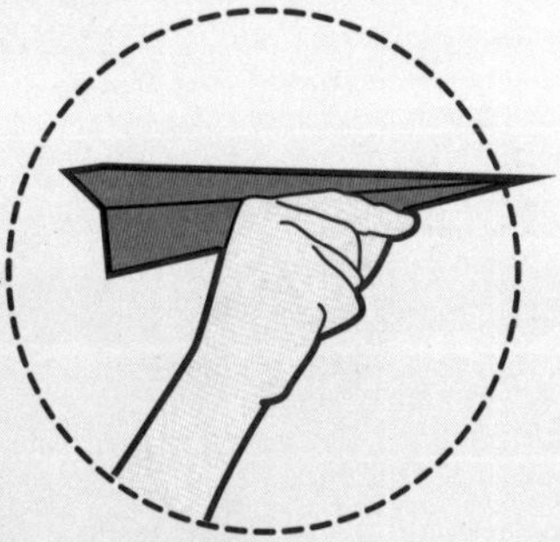

Folding

- Use a ruler to line up the folds and keep them sharp.
- If you want to keep your plane for another day, store it flat inside a book.
- If your paper plane gets wet, or won't fly... fold a new one!

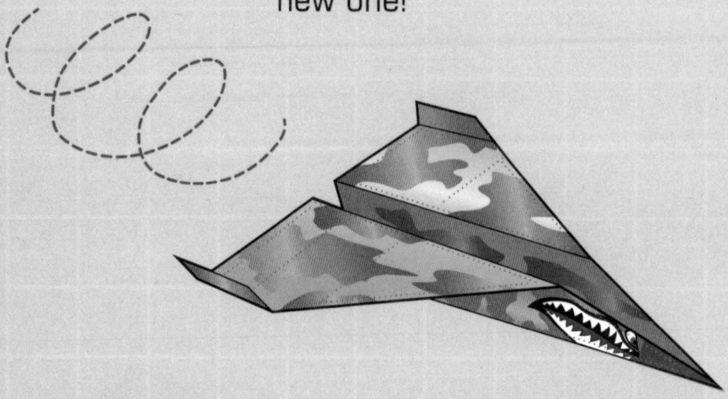

Flying

- Try changing the angle of your plane's wings to alter its flight.

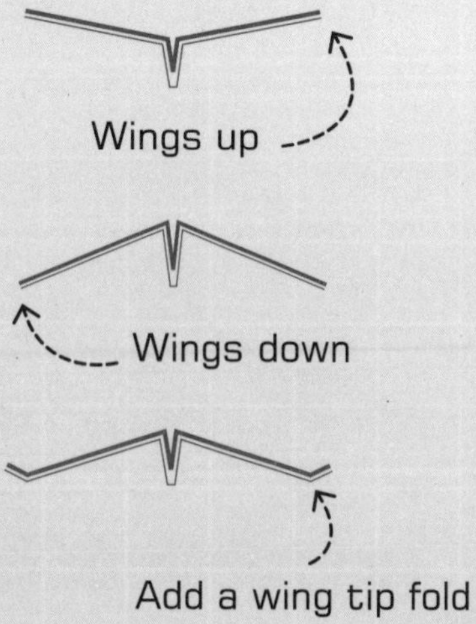

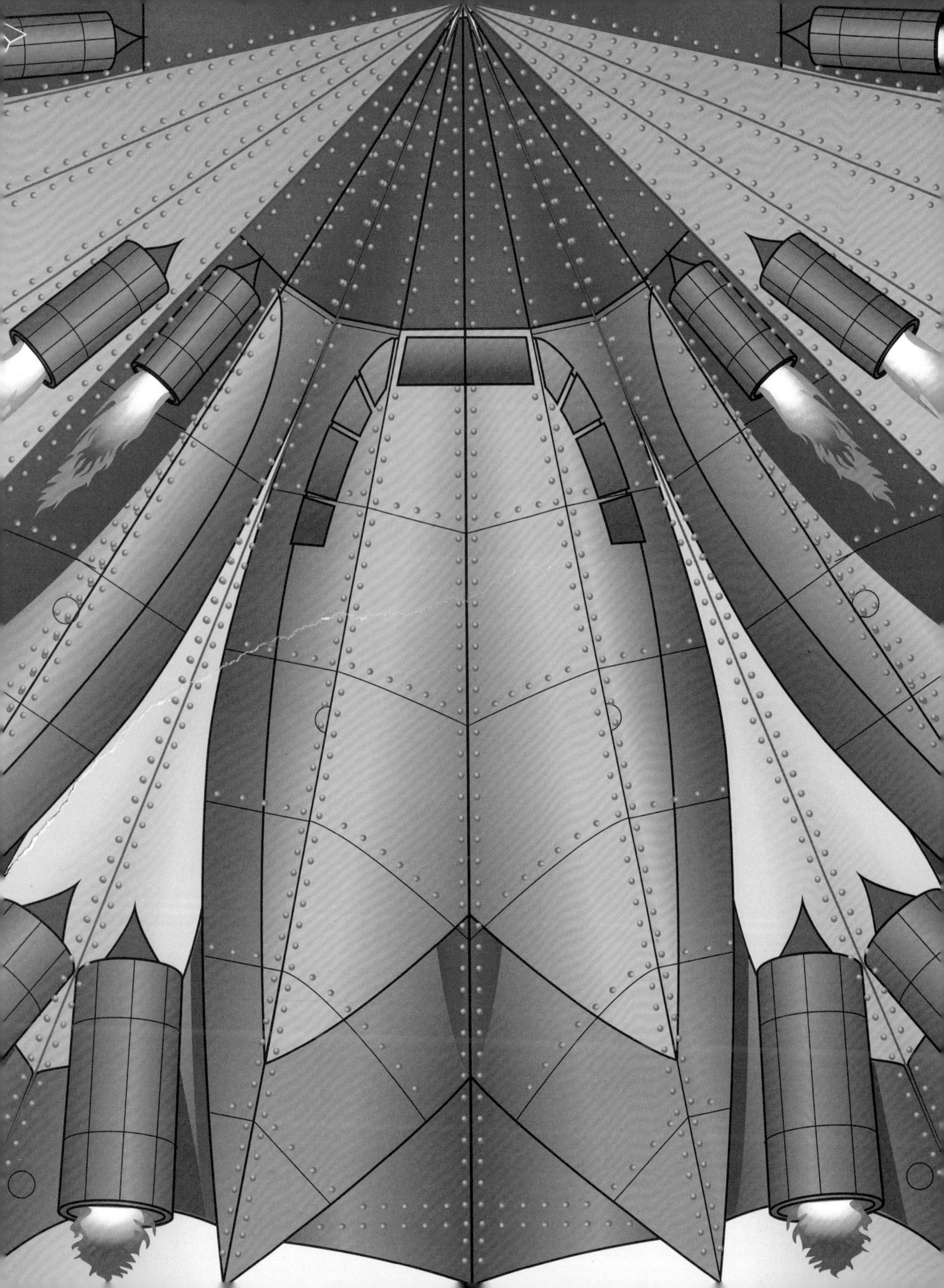

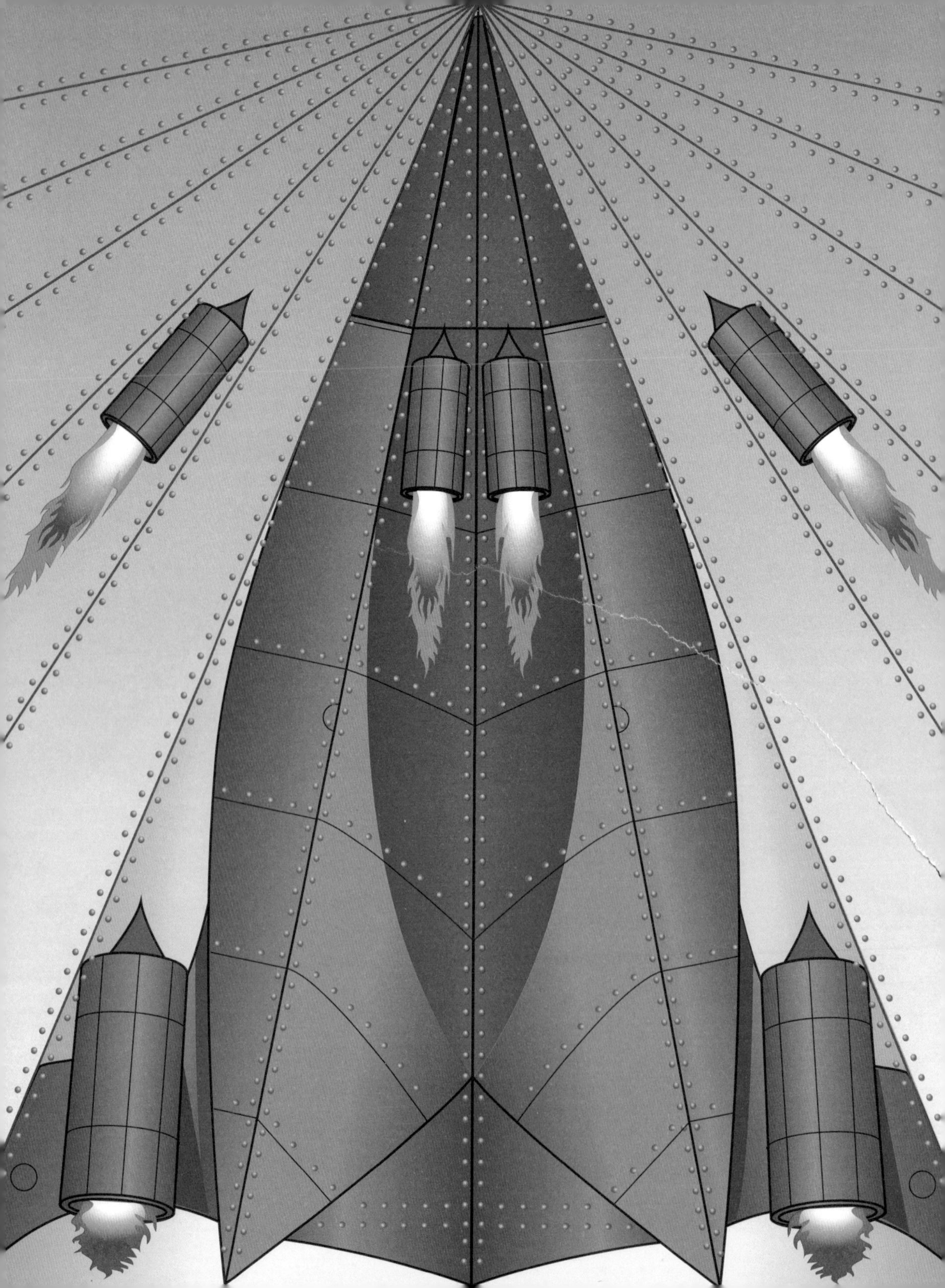

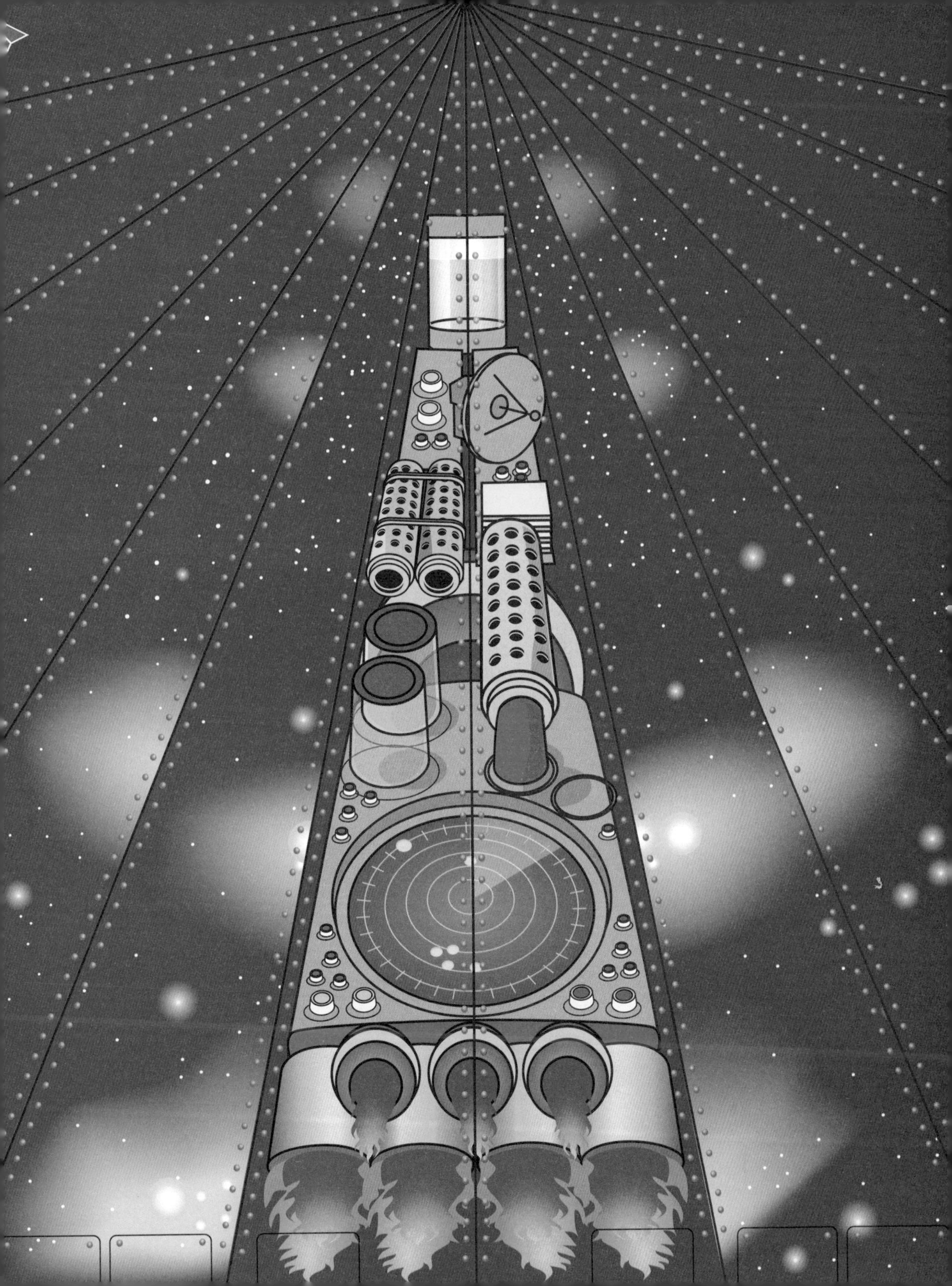

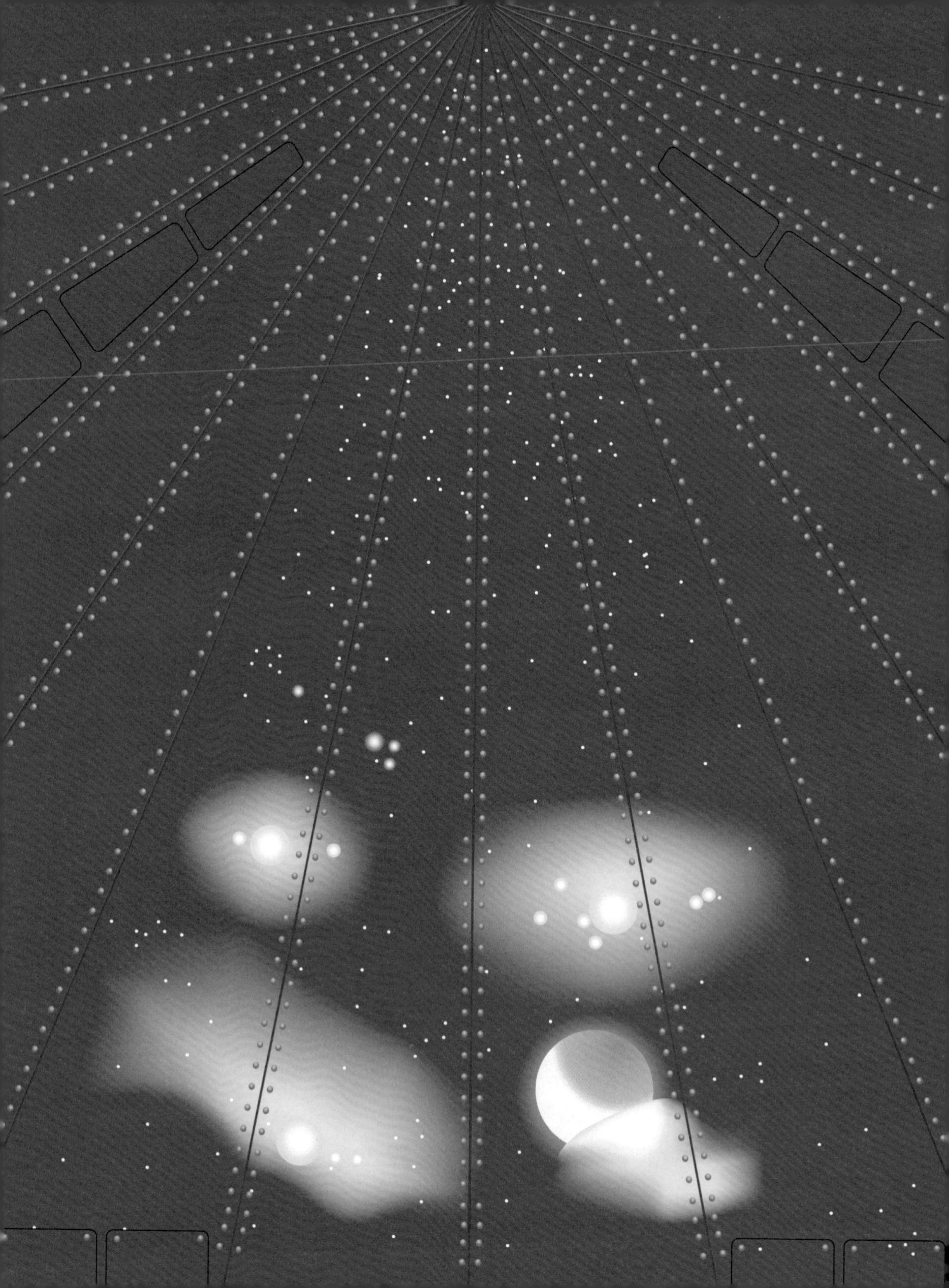

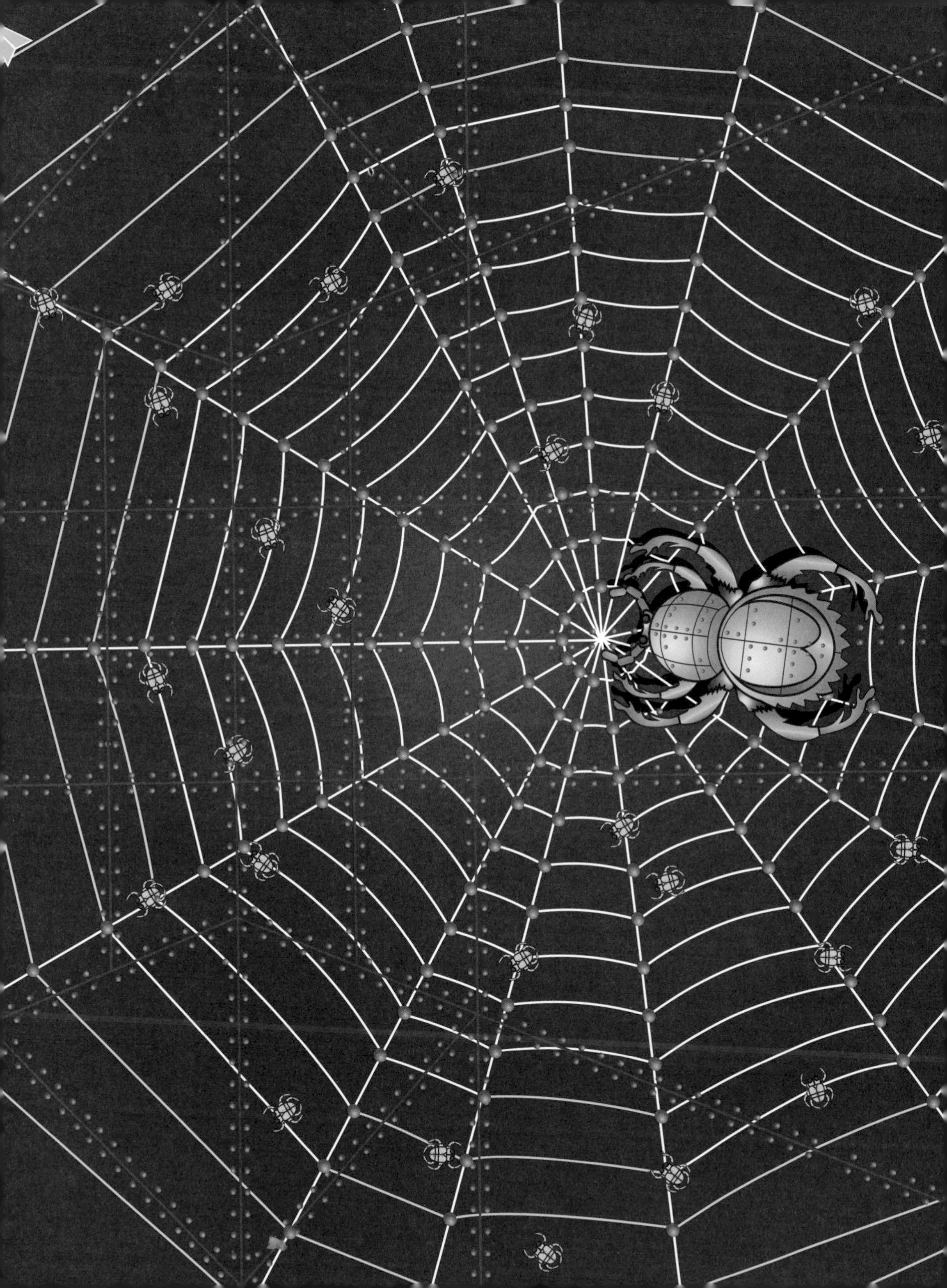

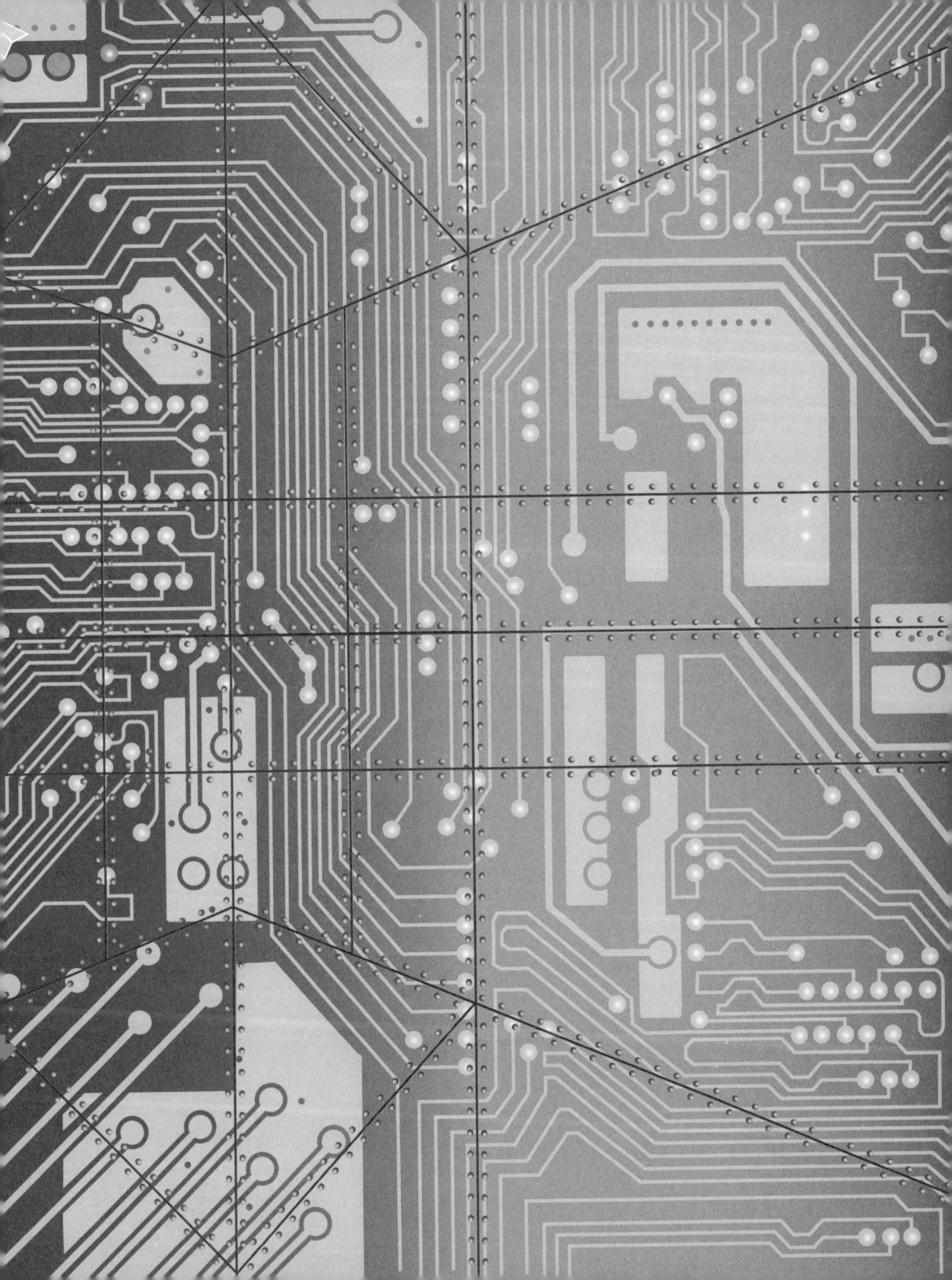

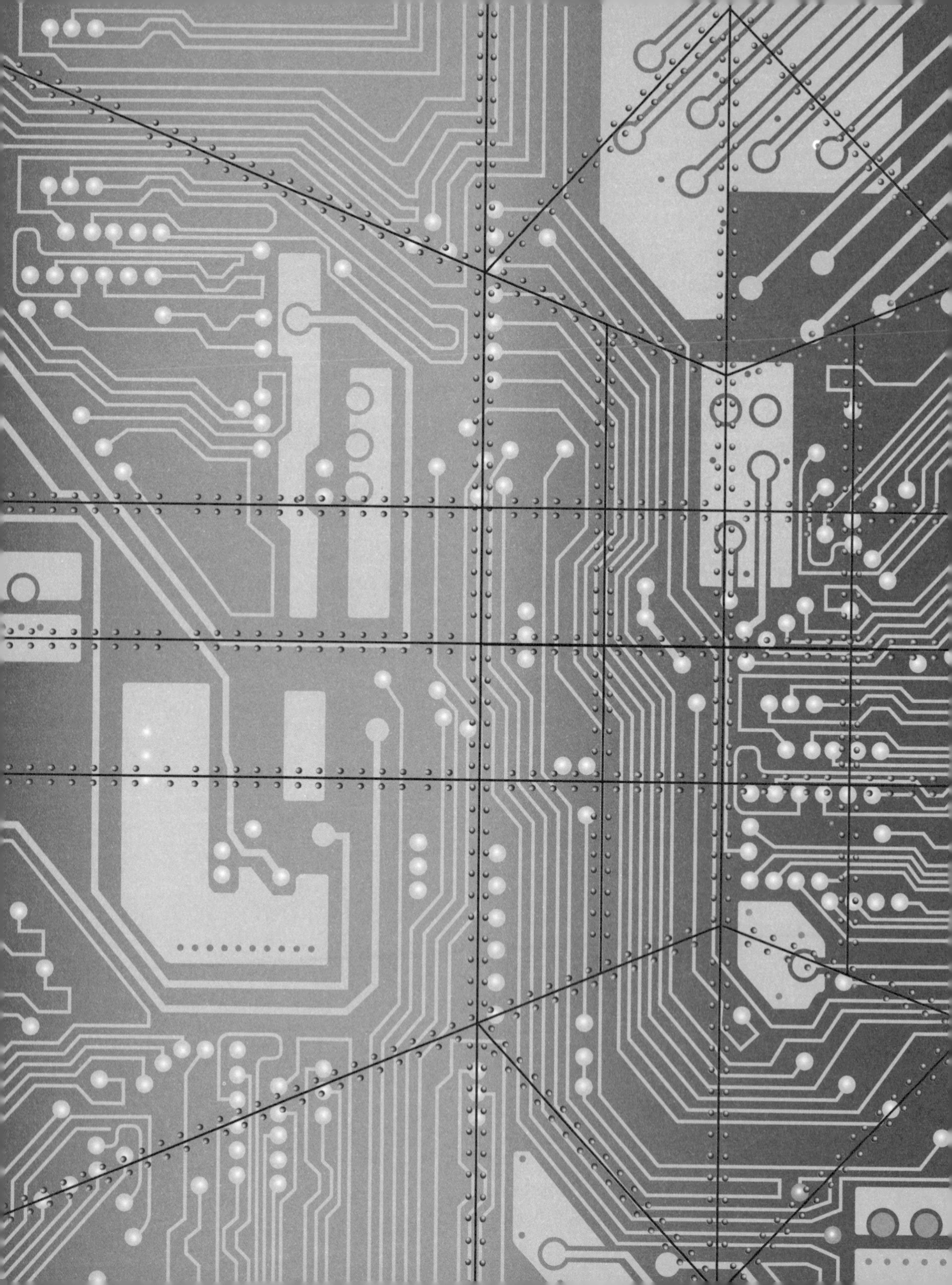

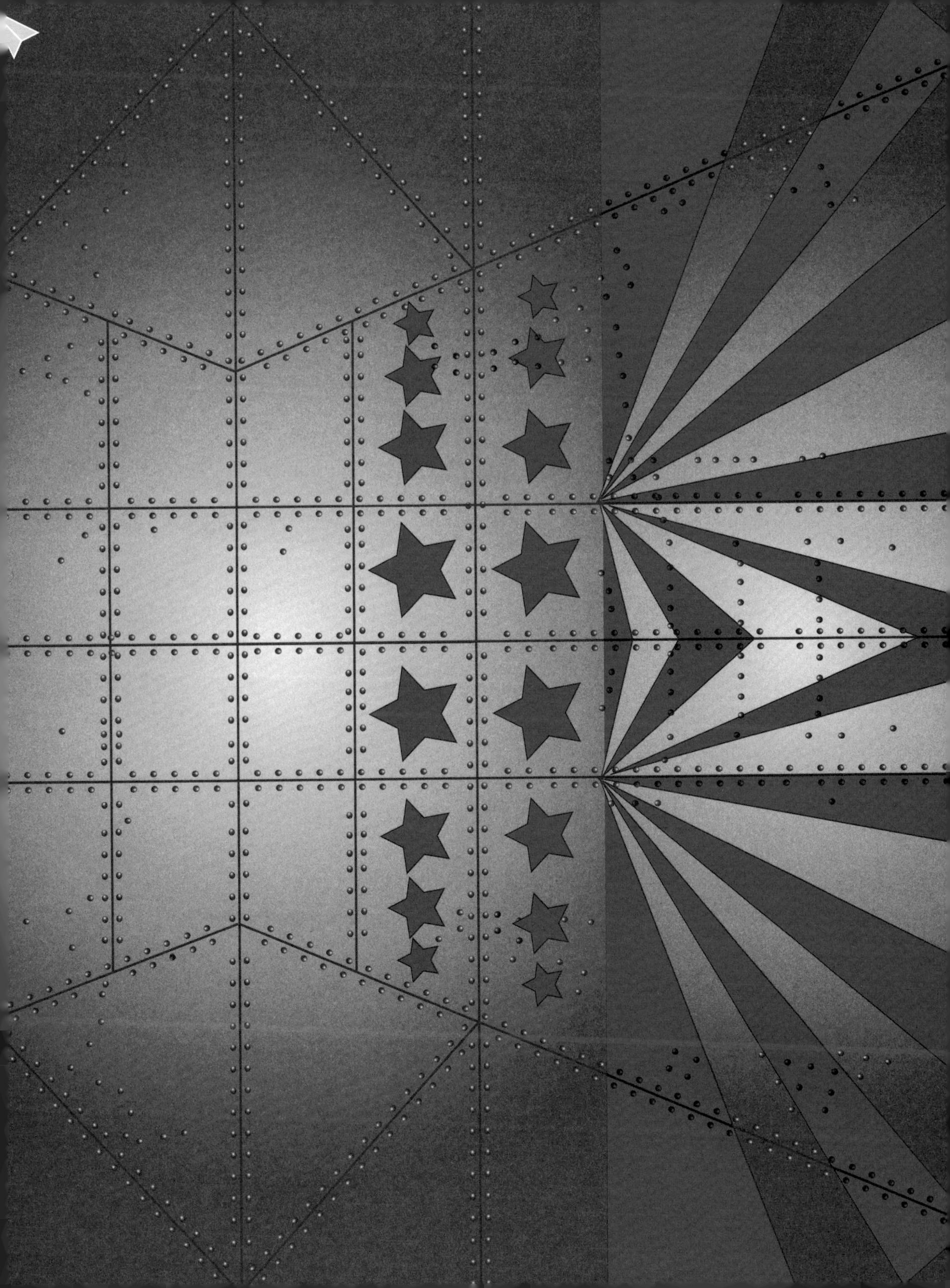

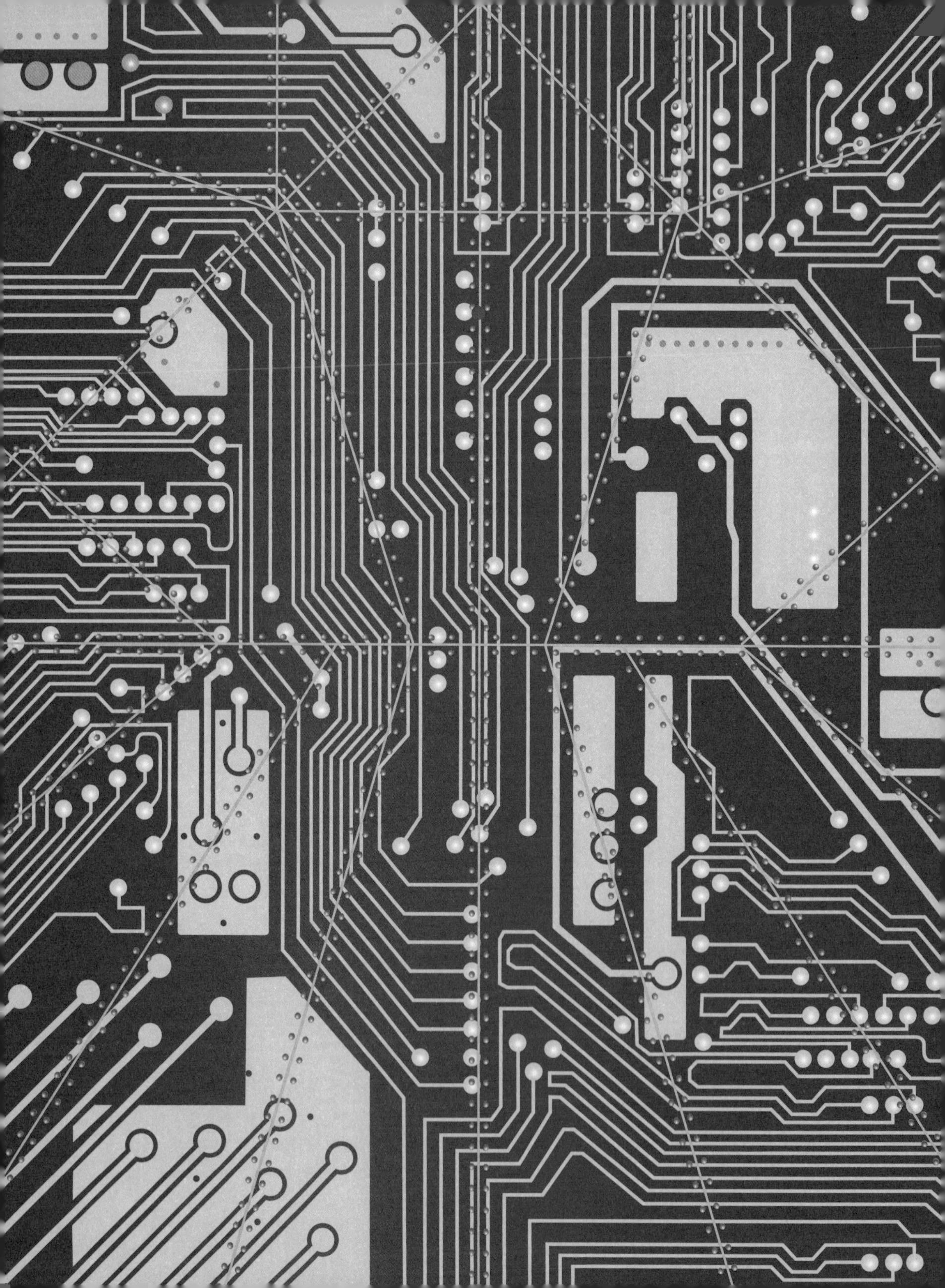

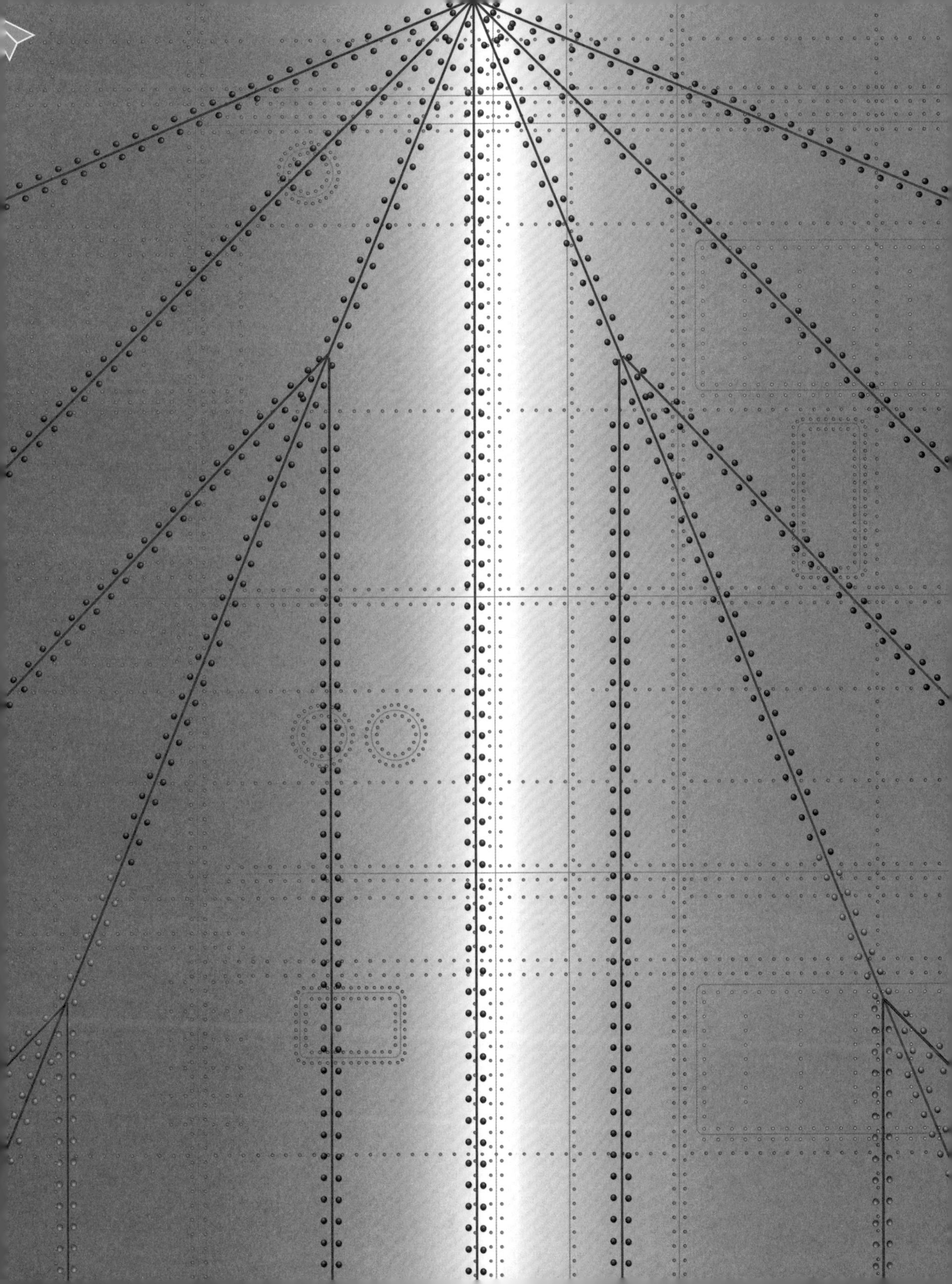

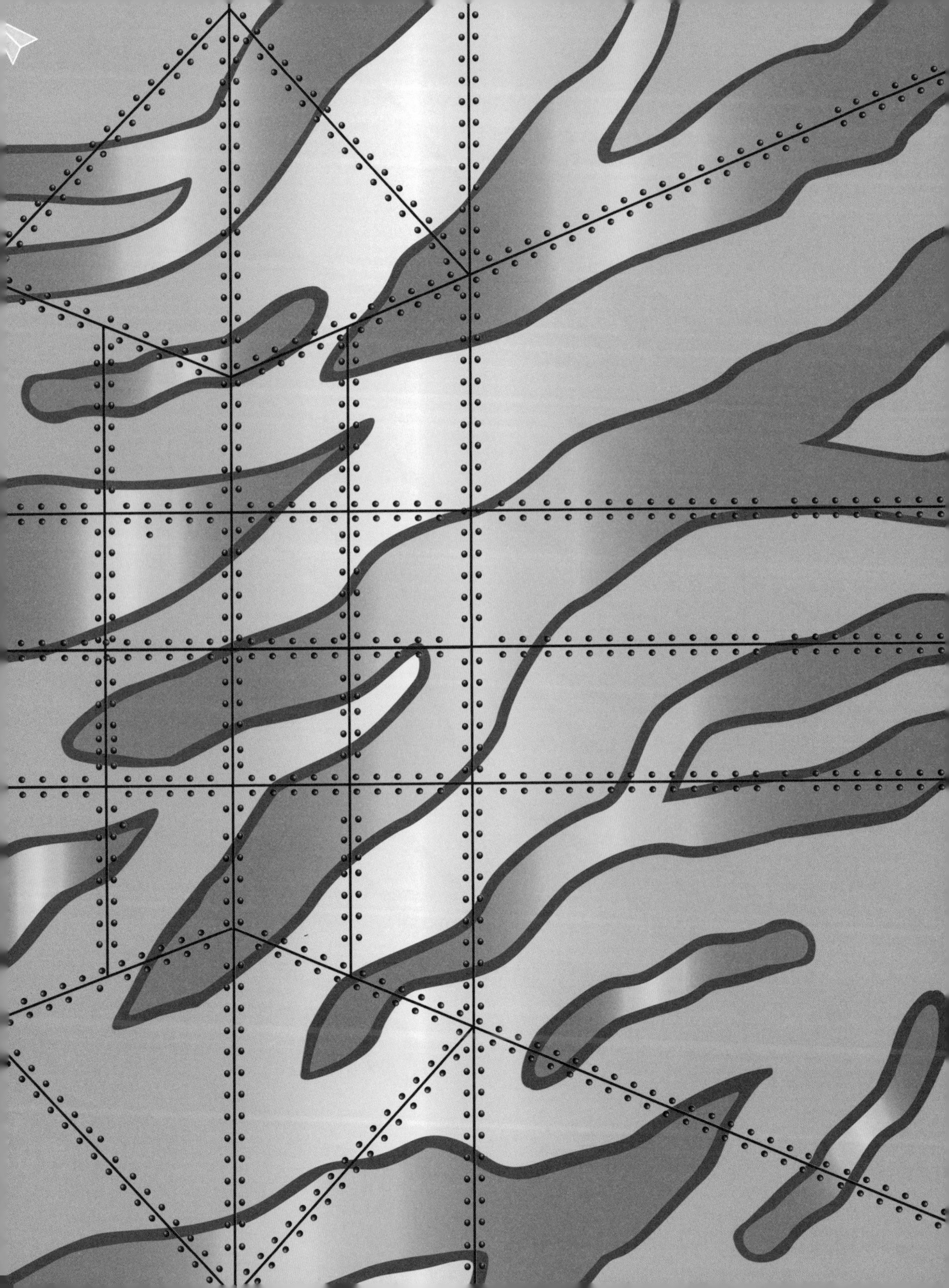

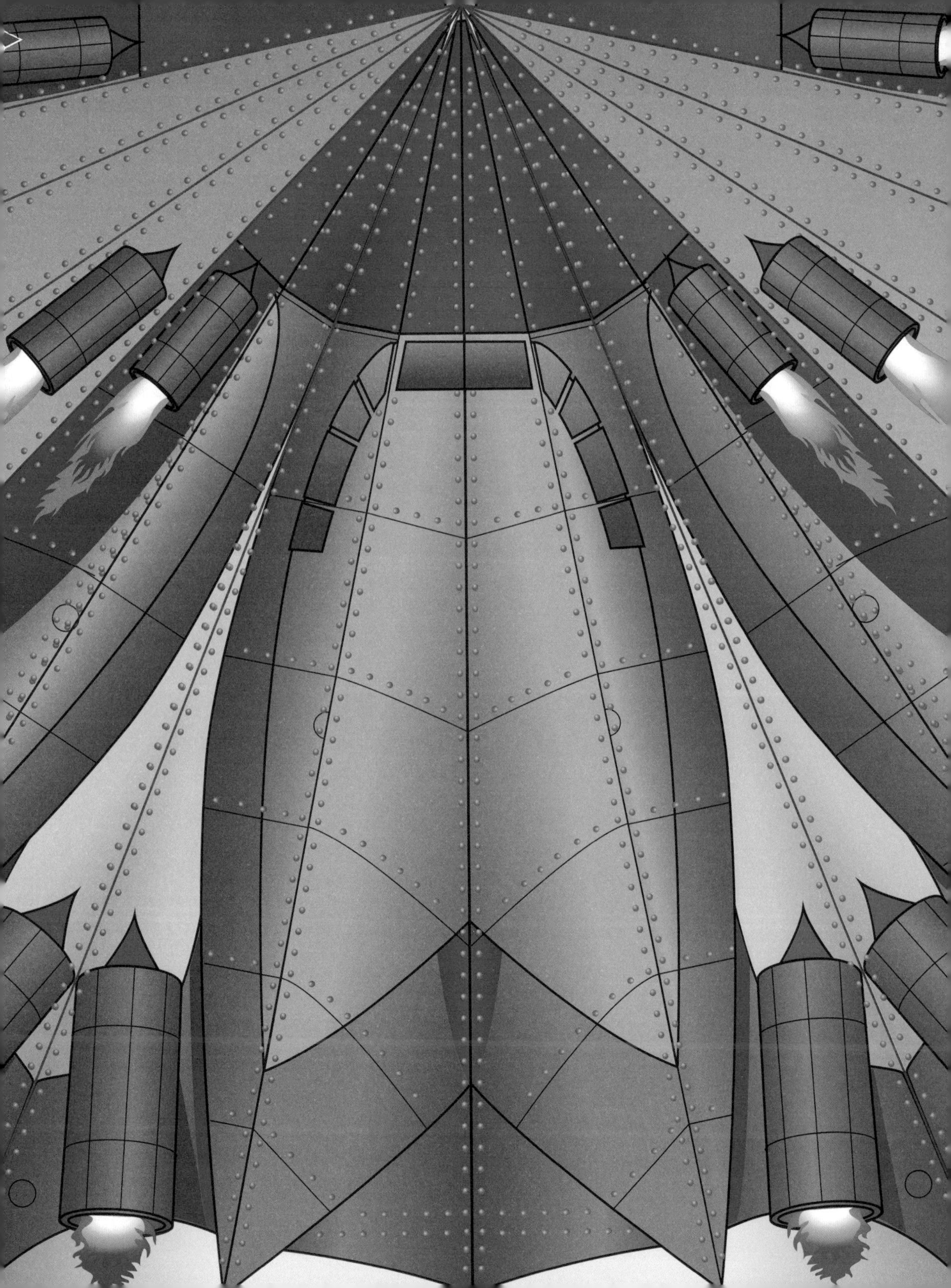

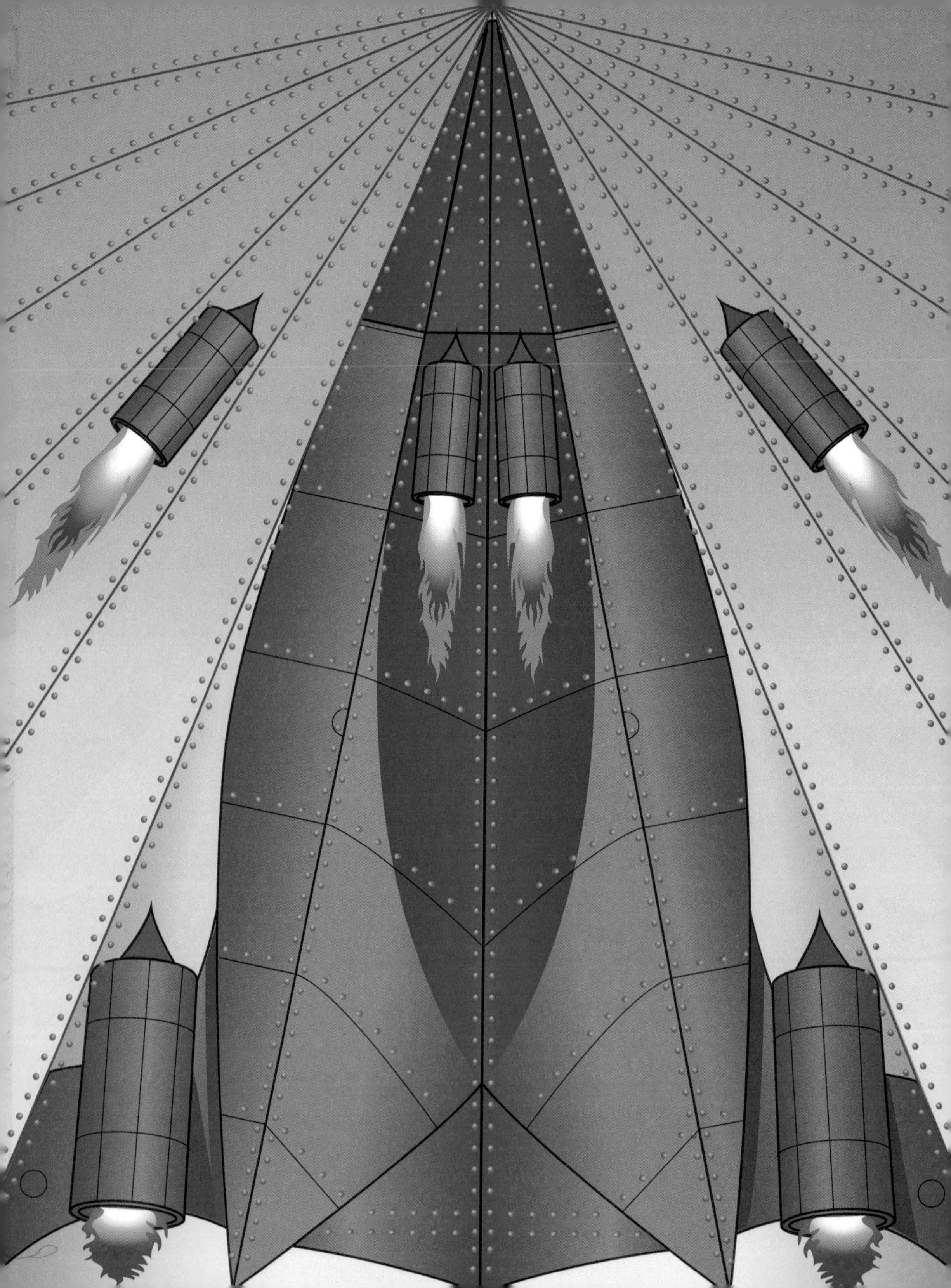

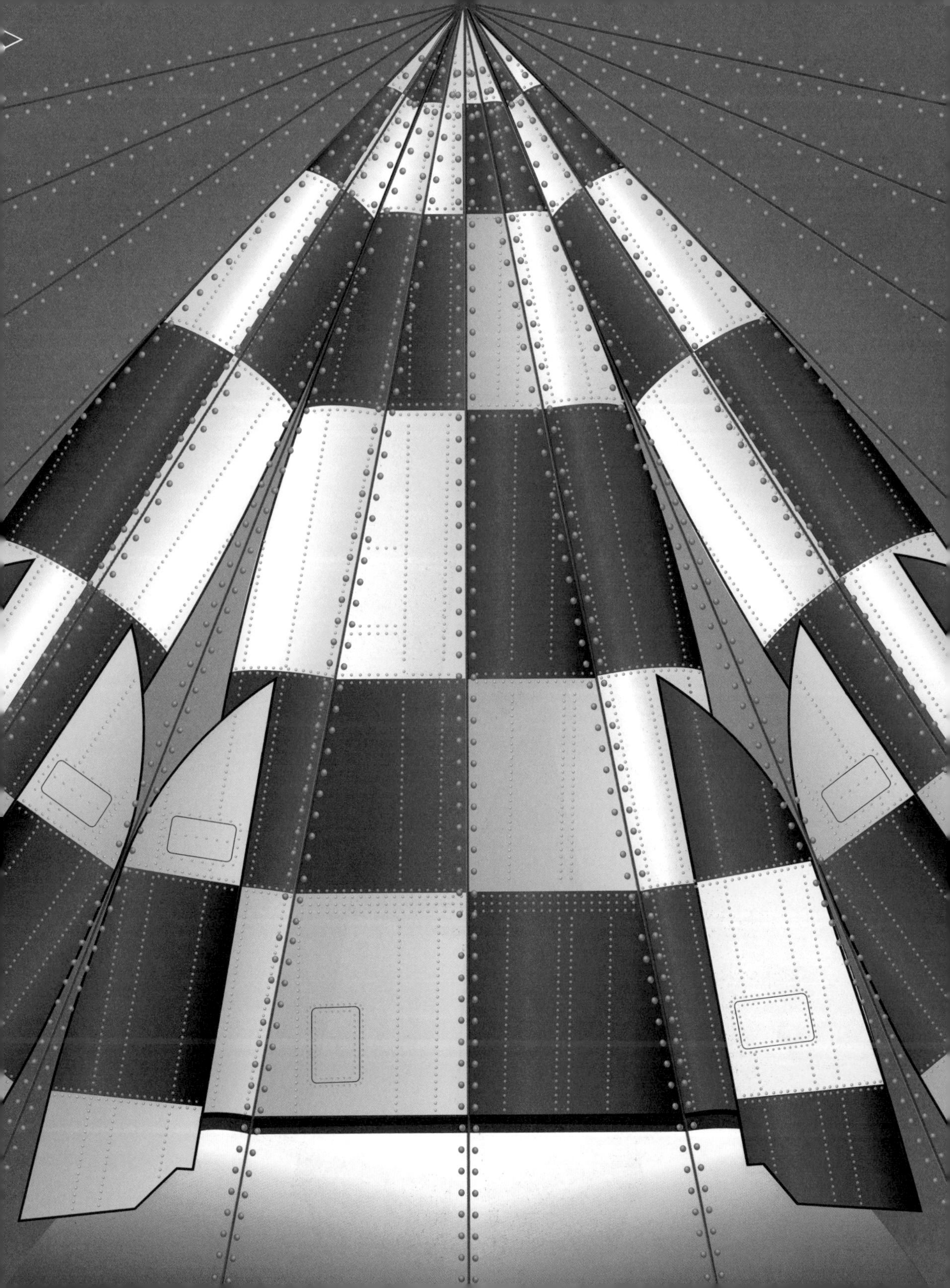

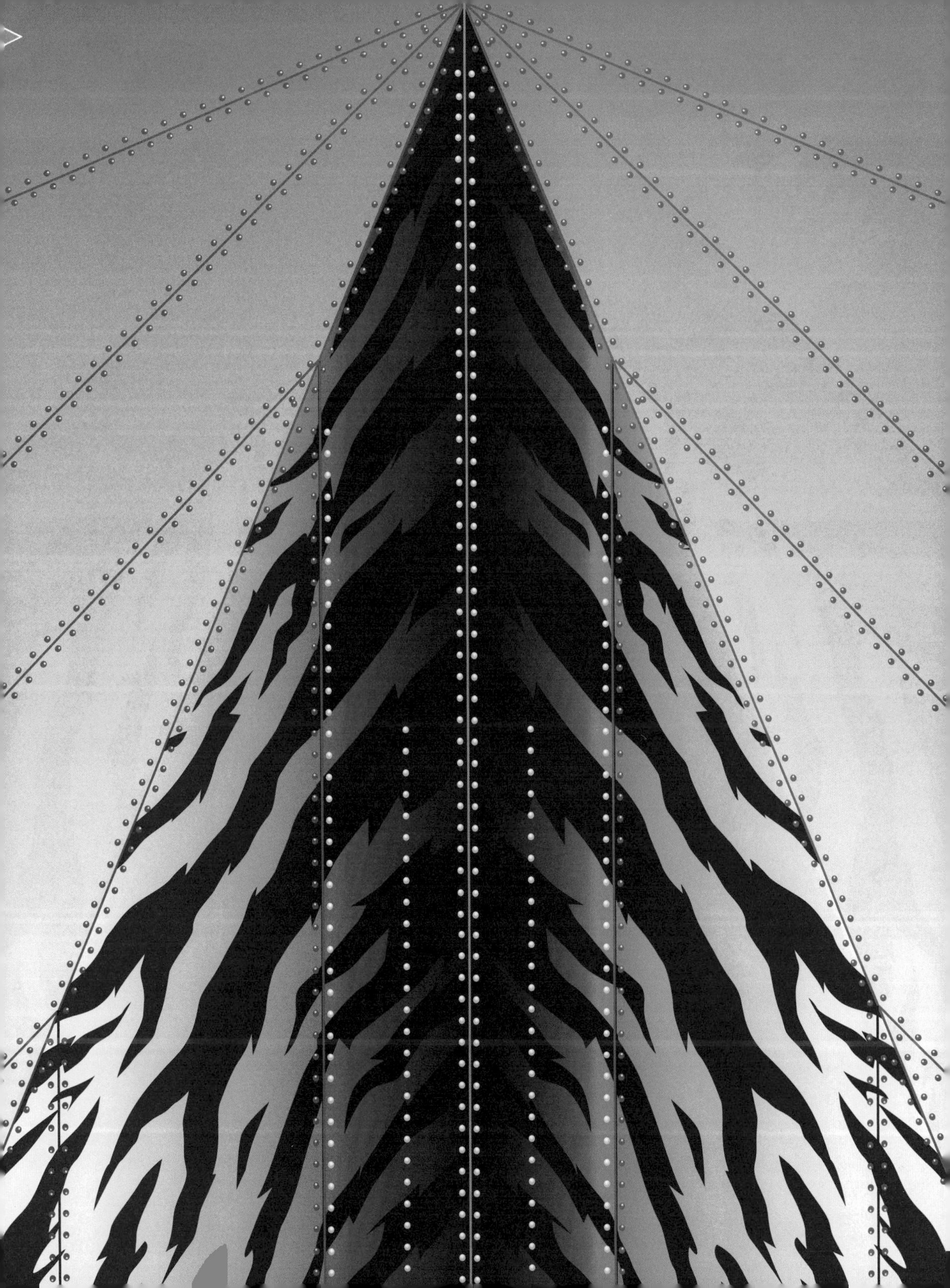

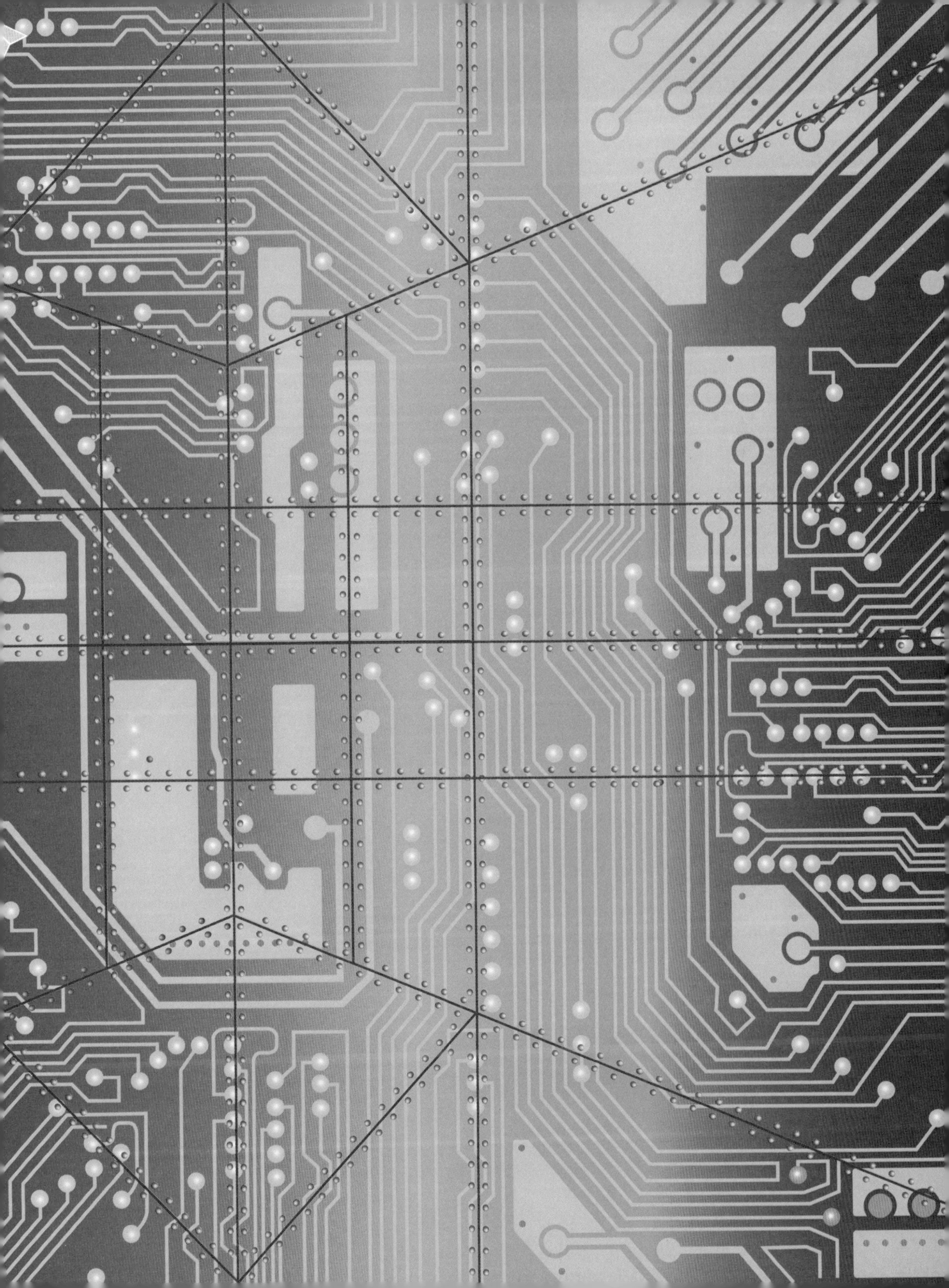

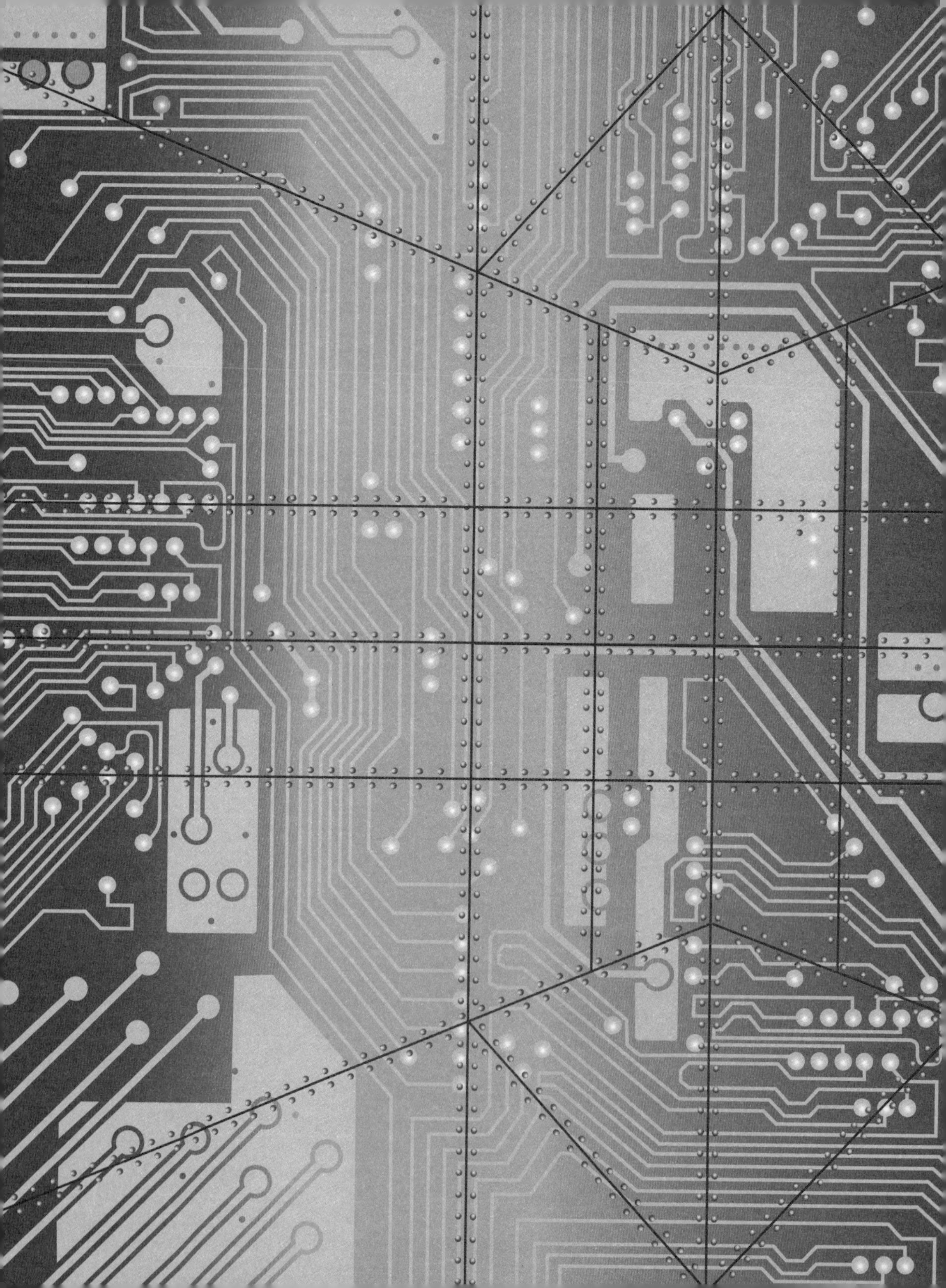

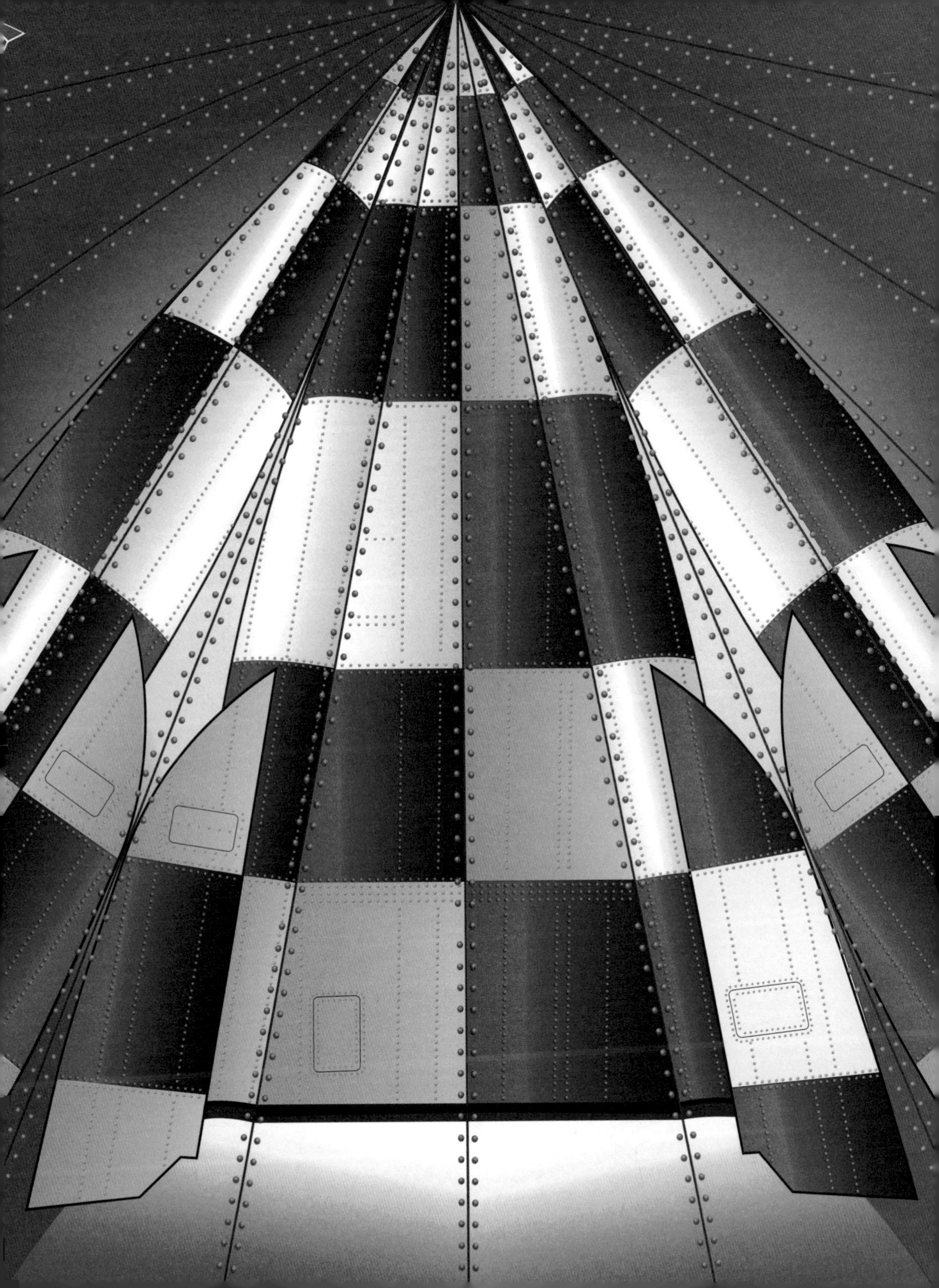

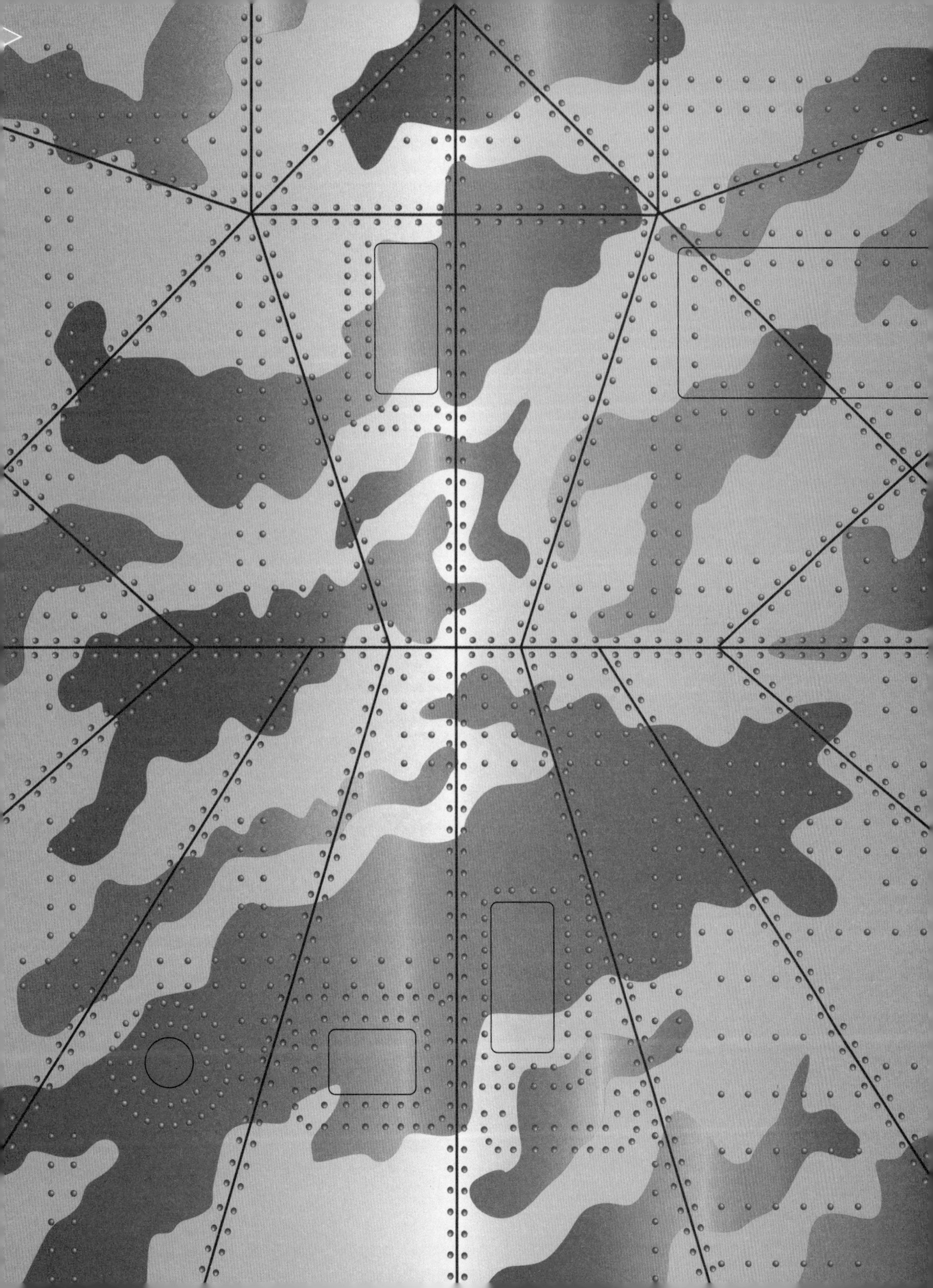

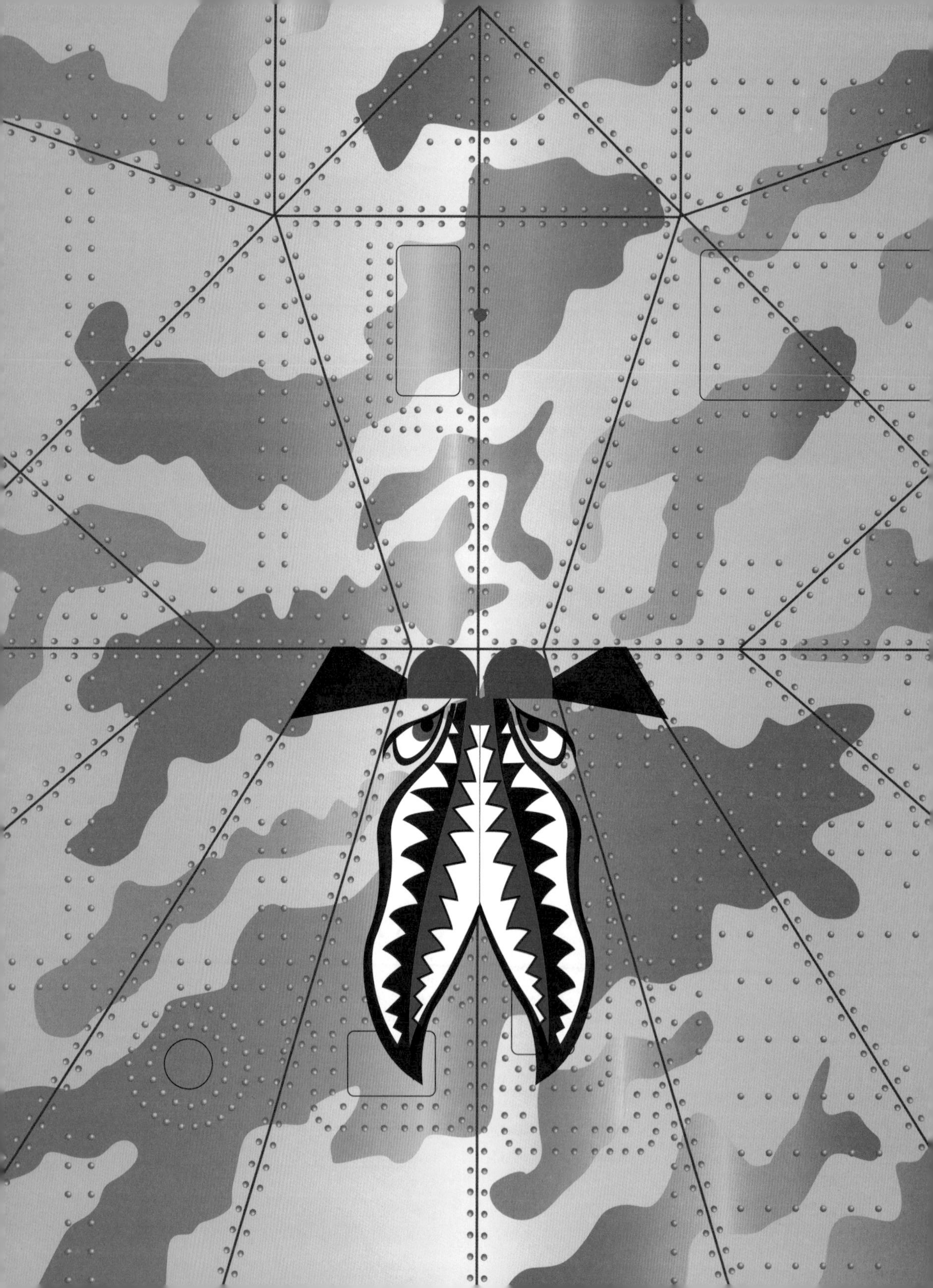

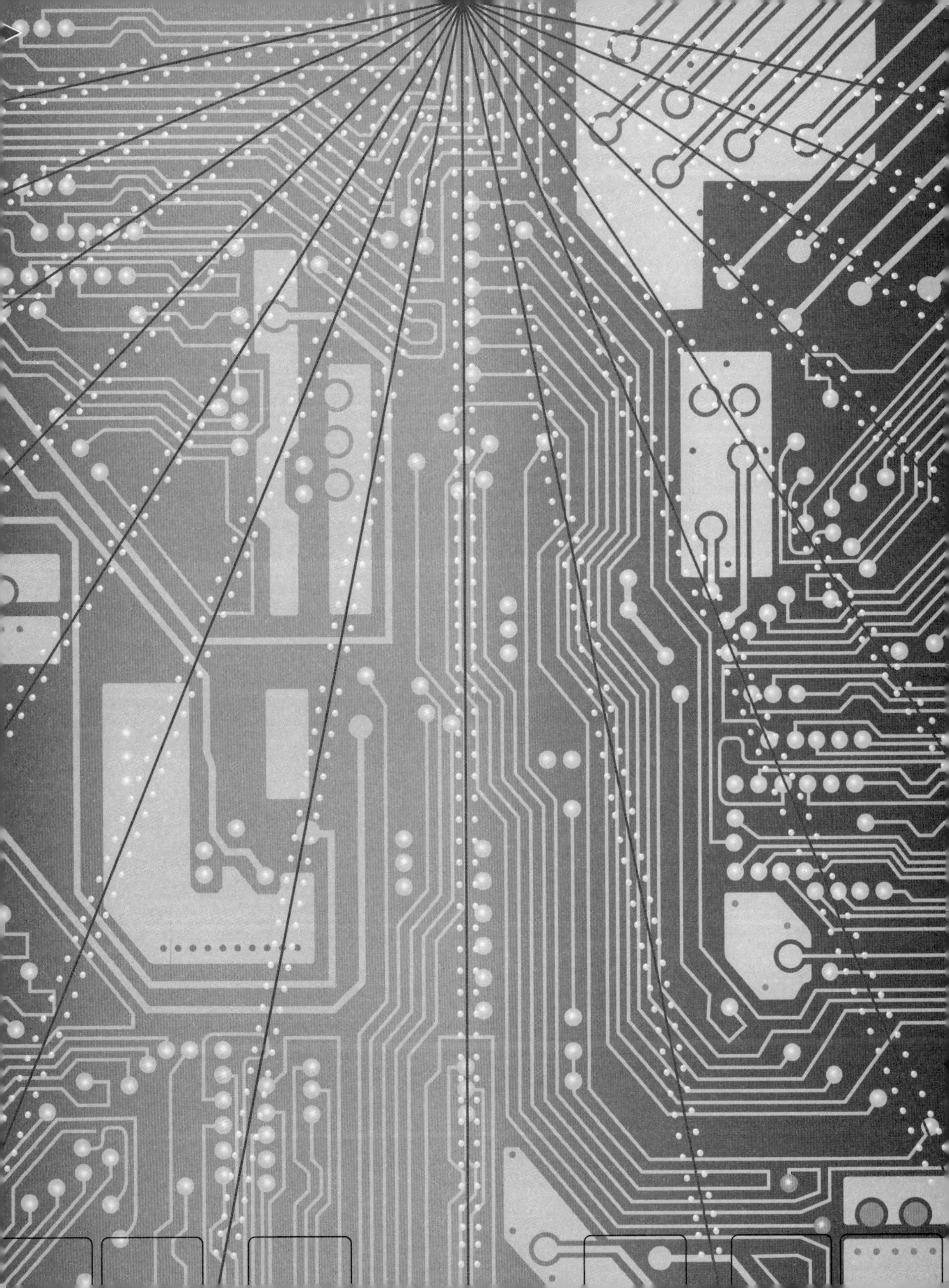

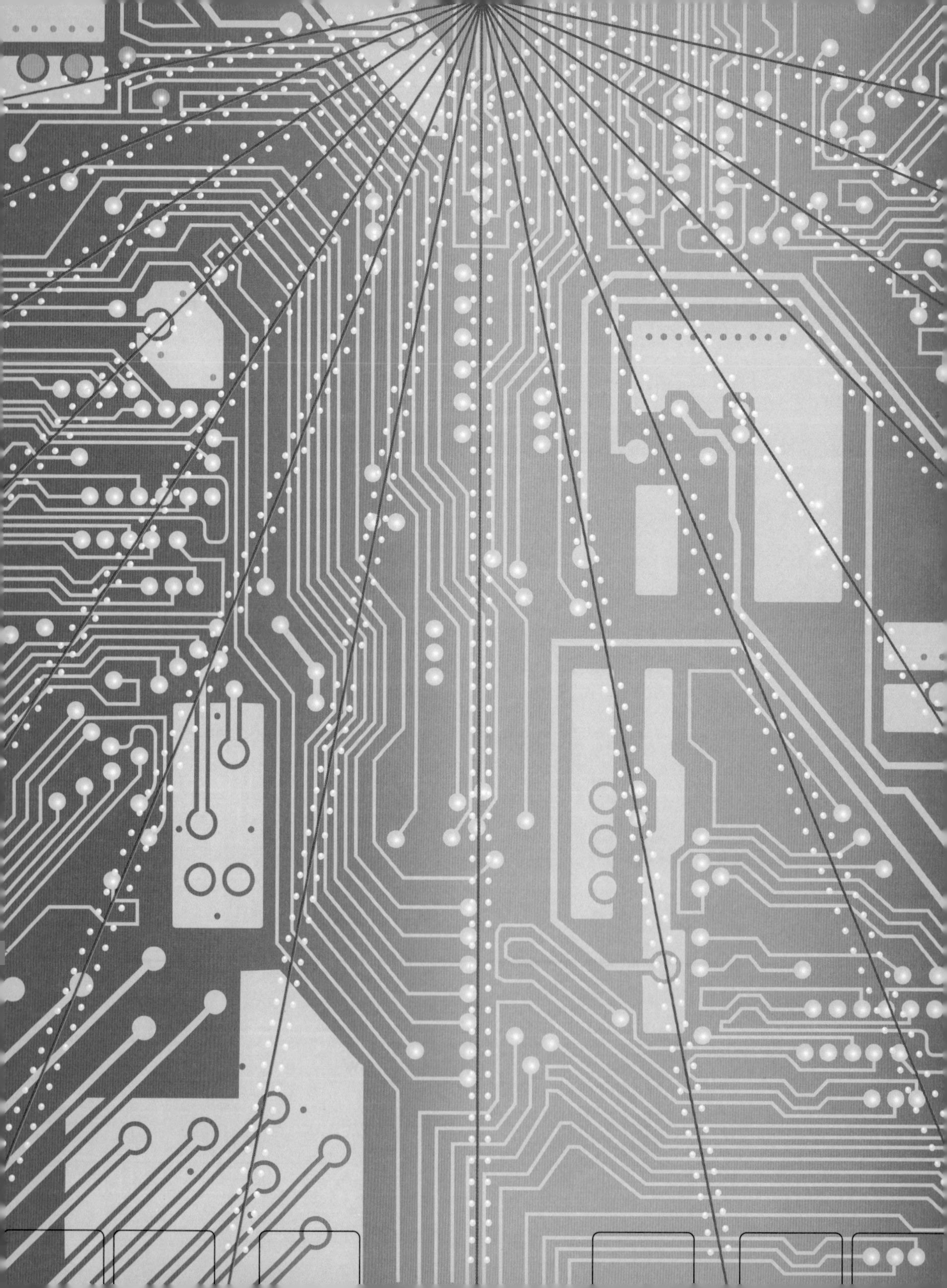

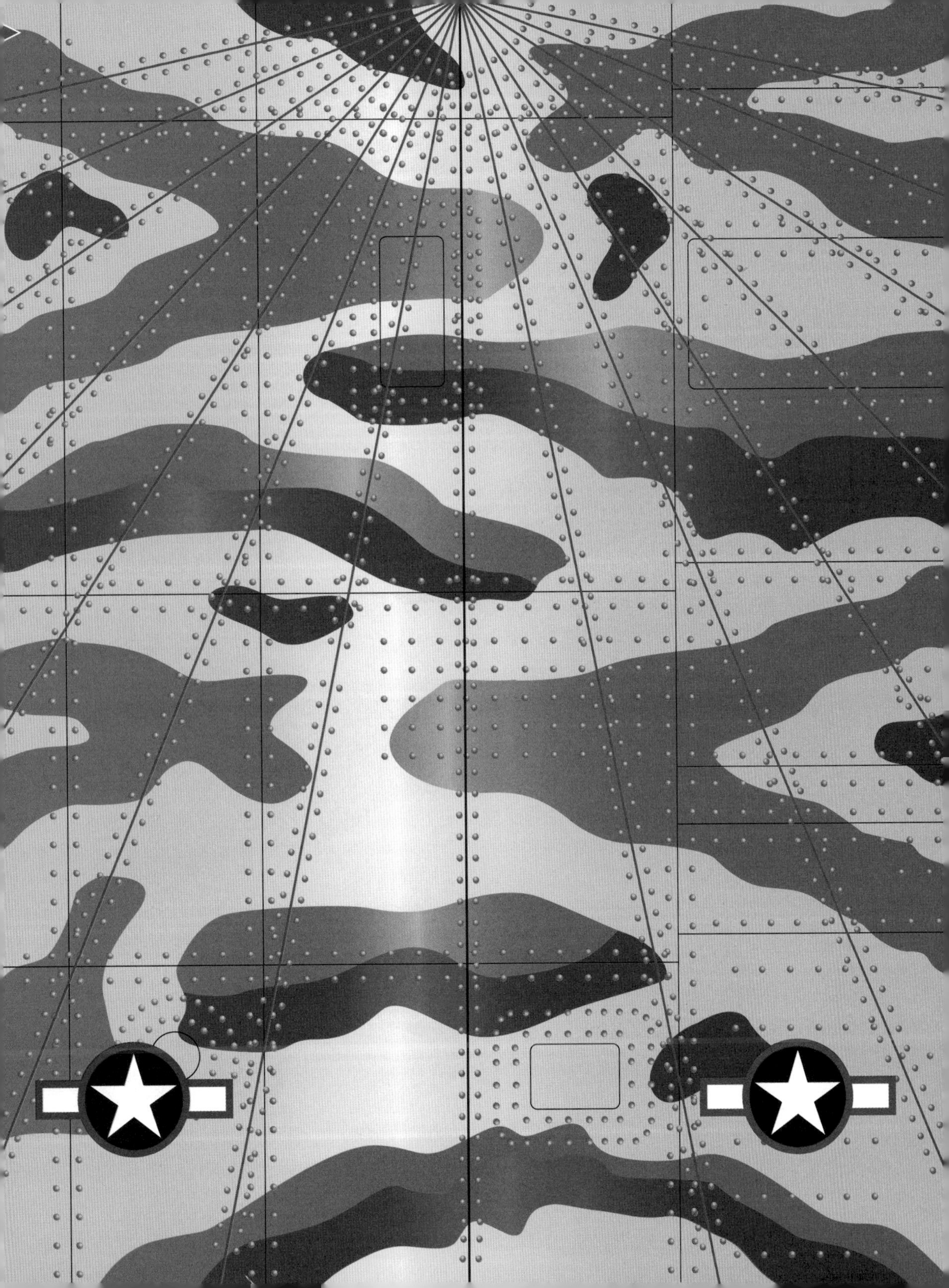

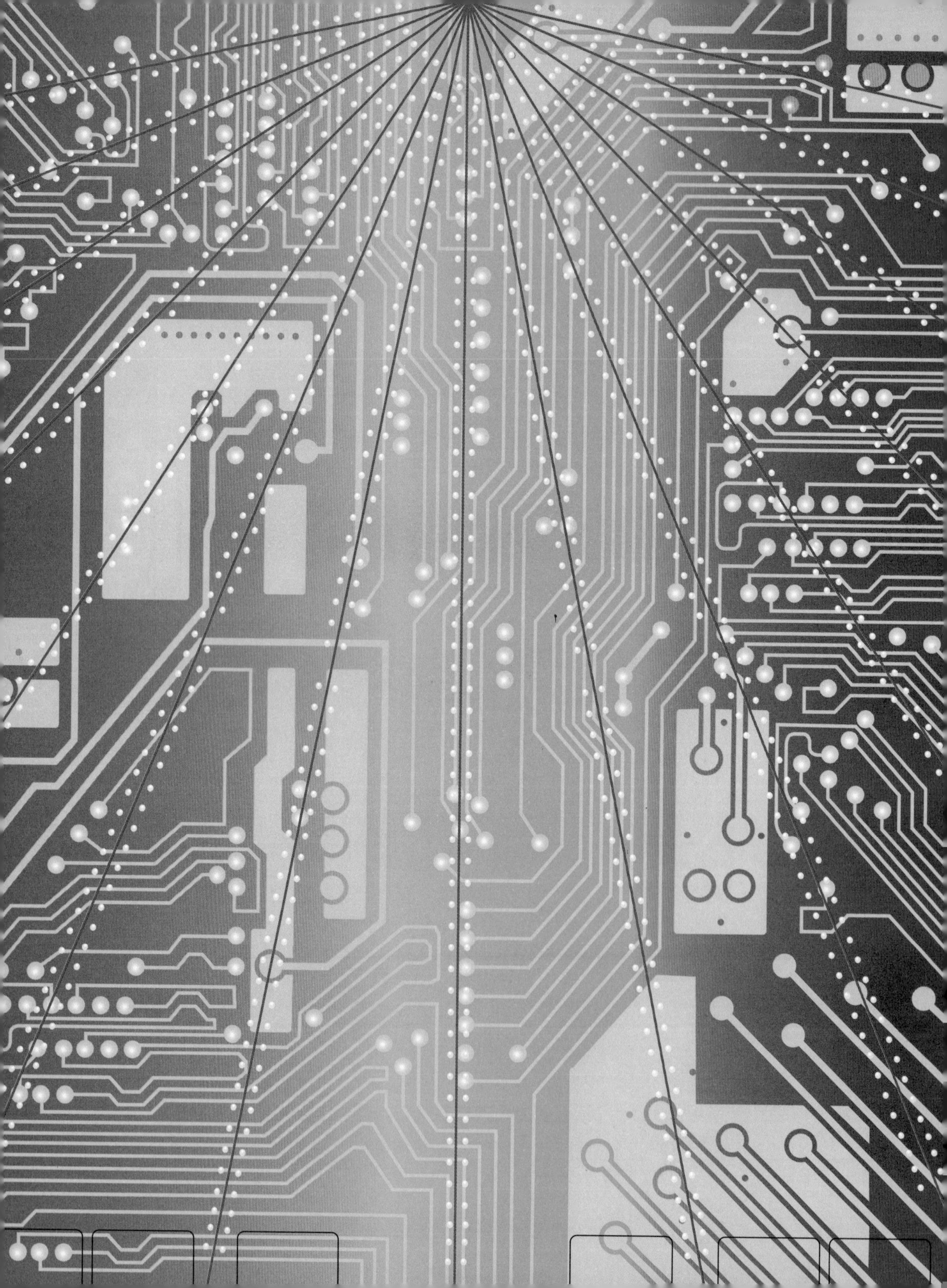

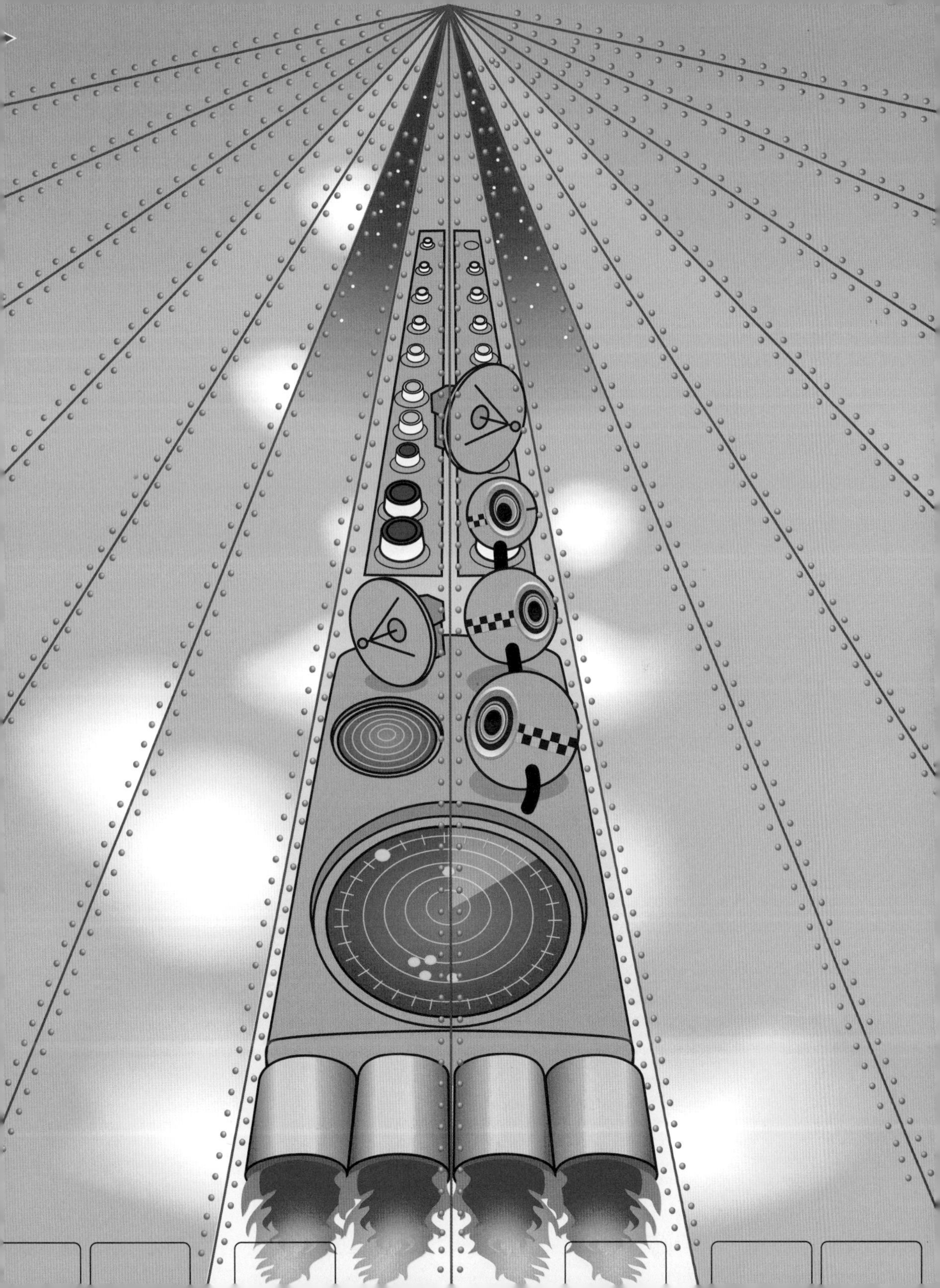

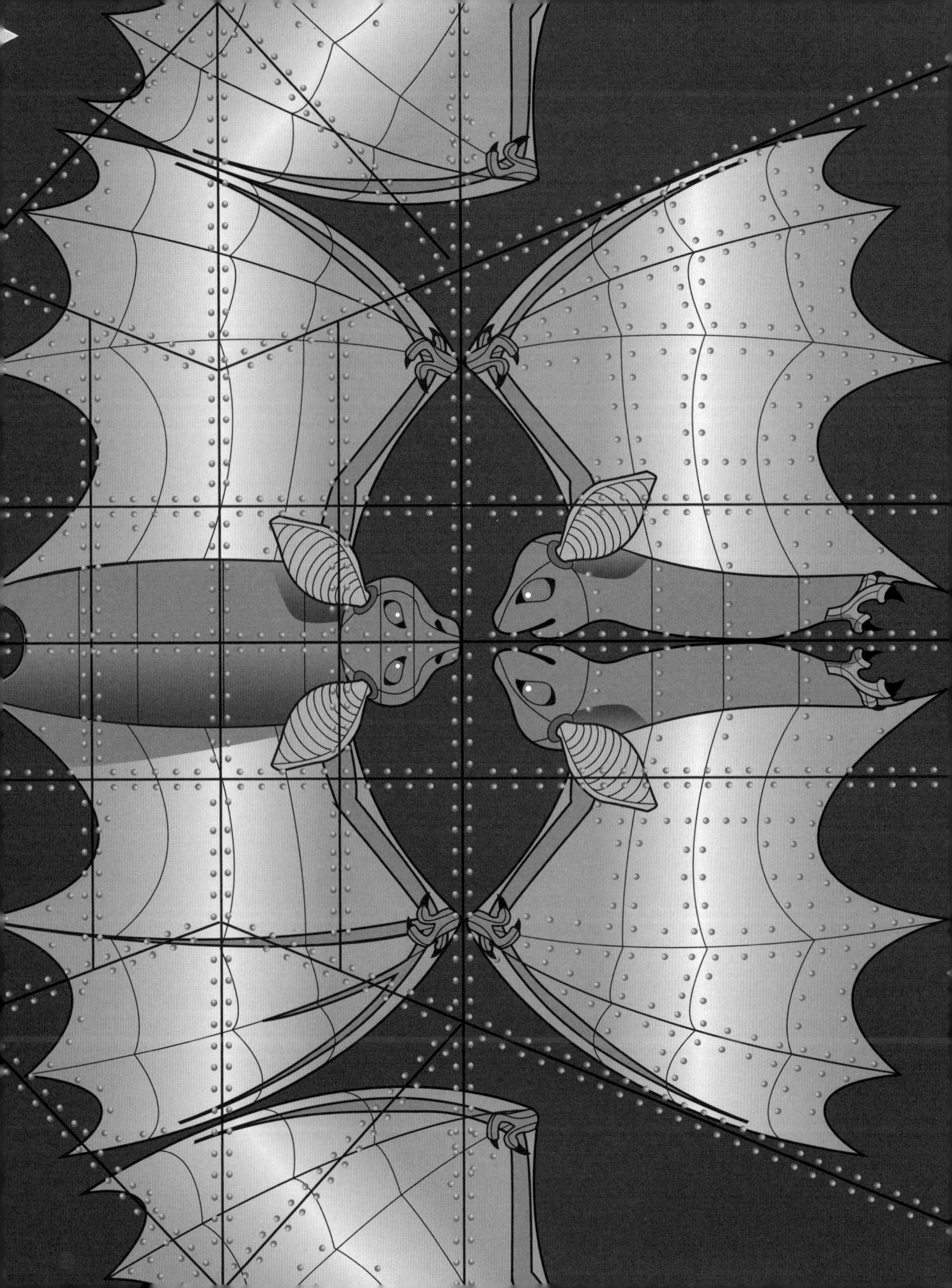

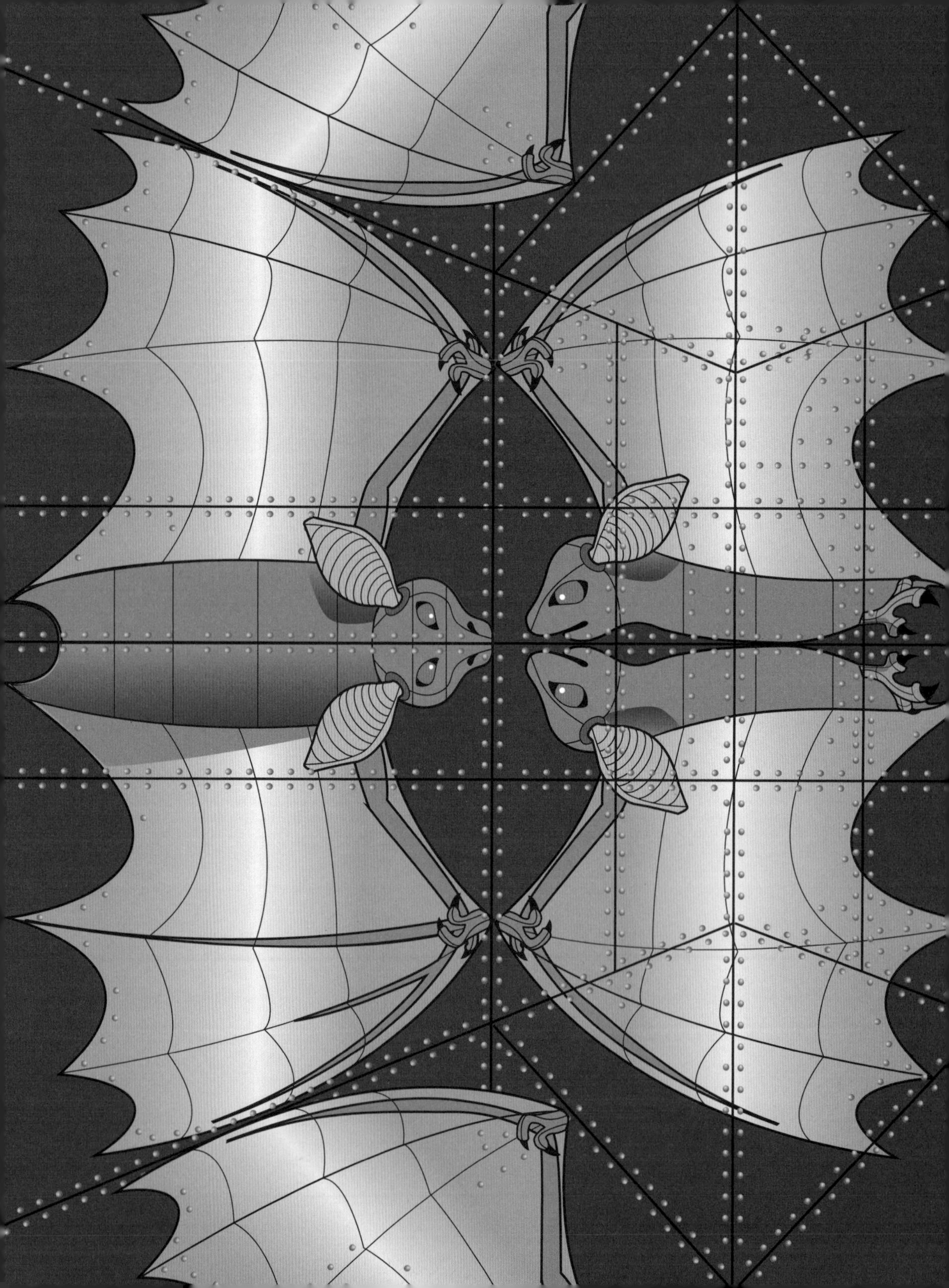

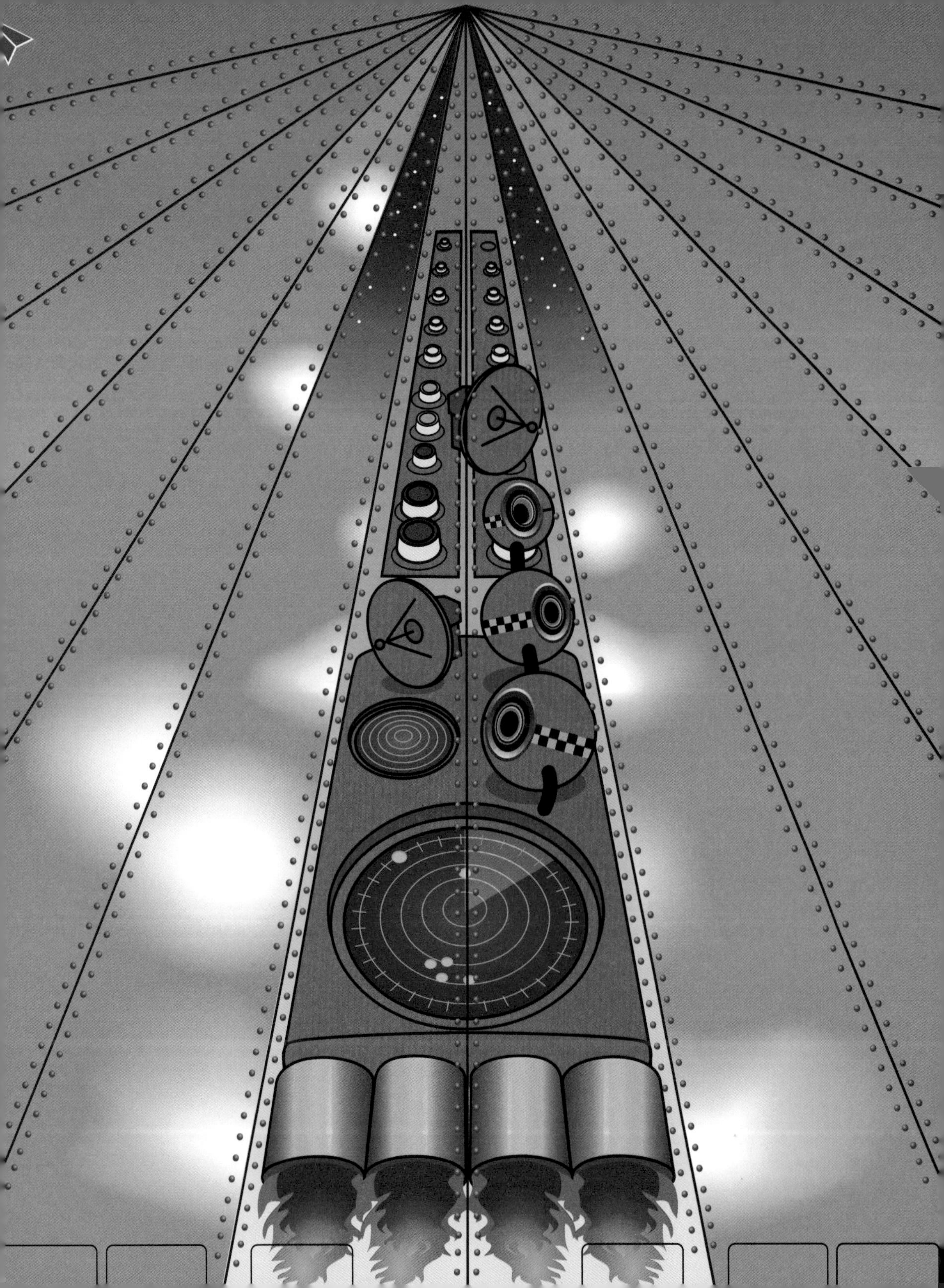

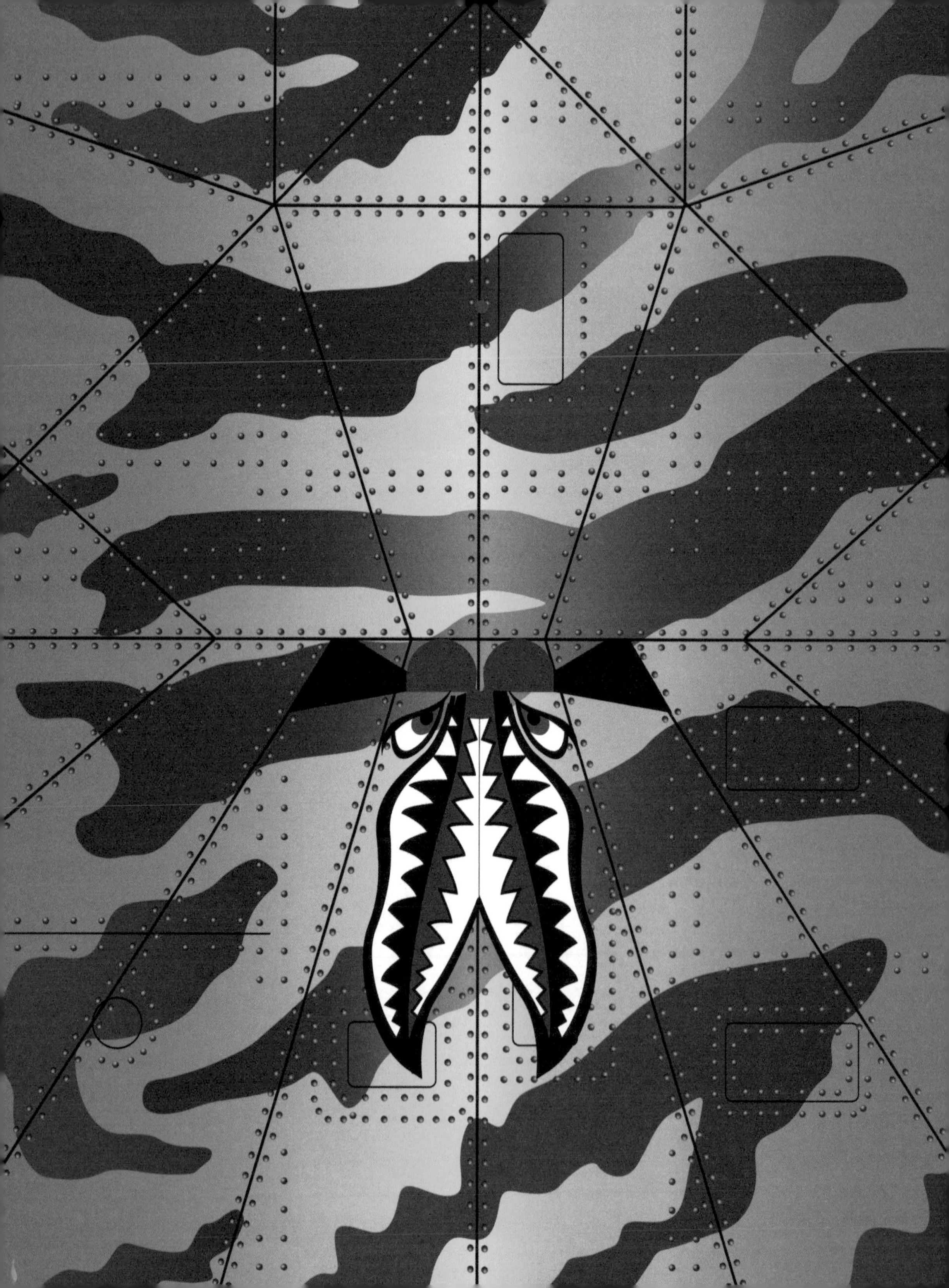

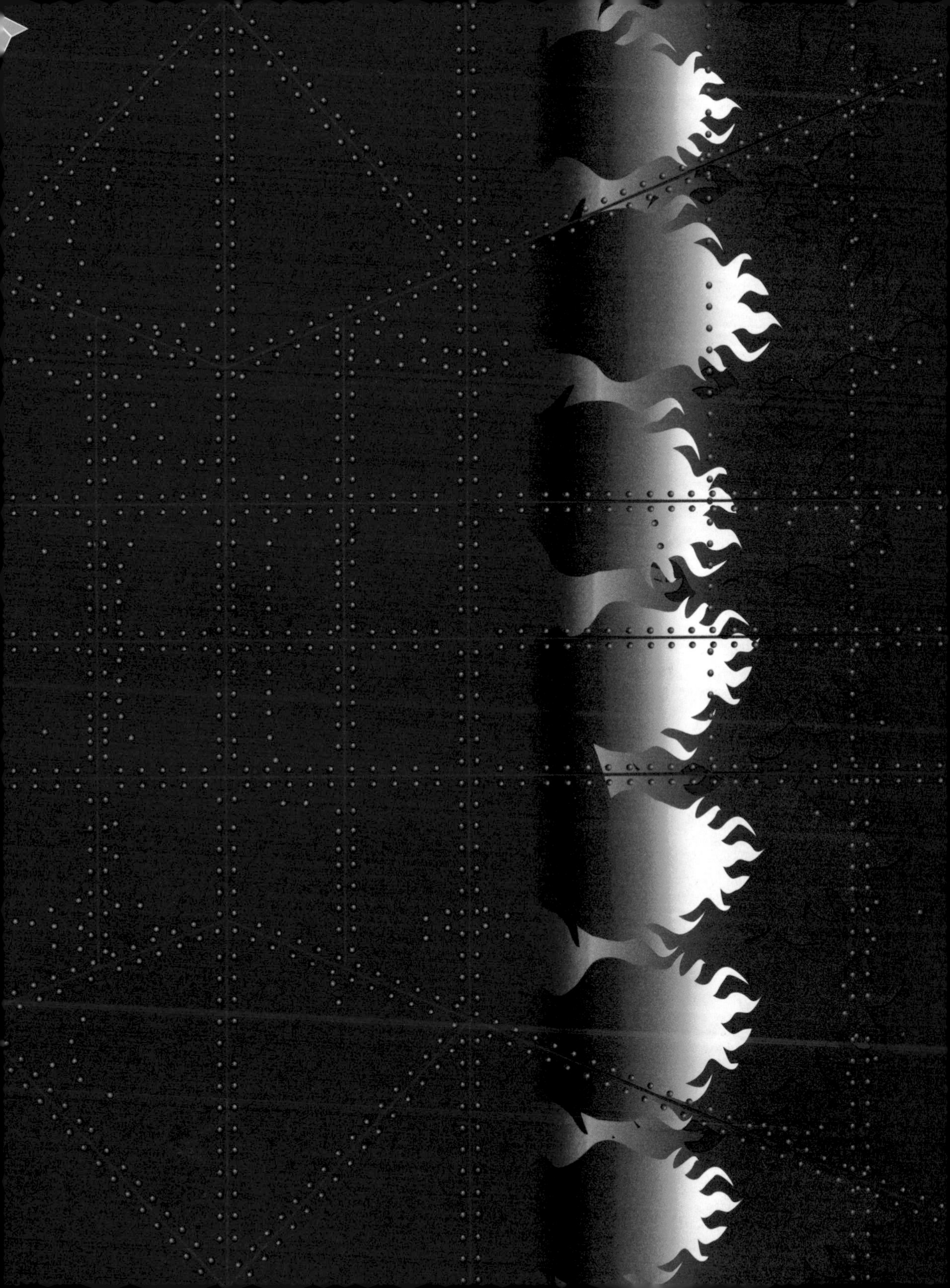

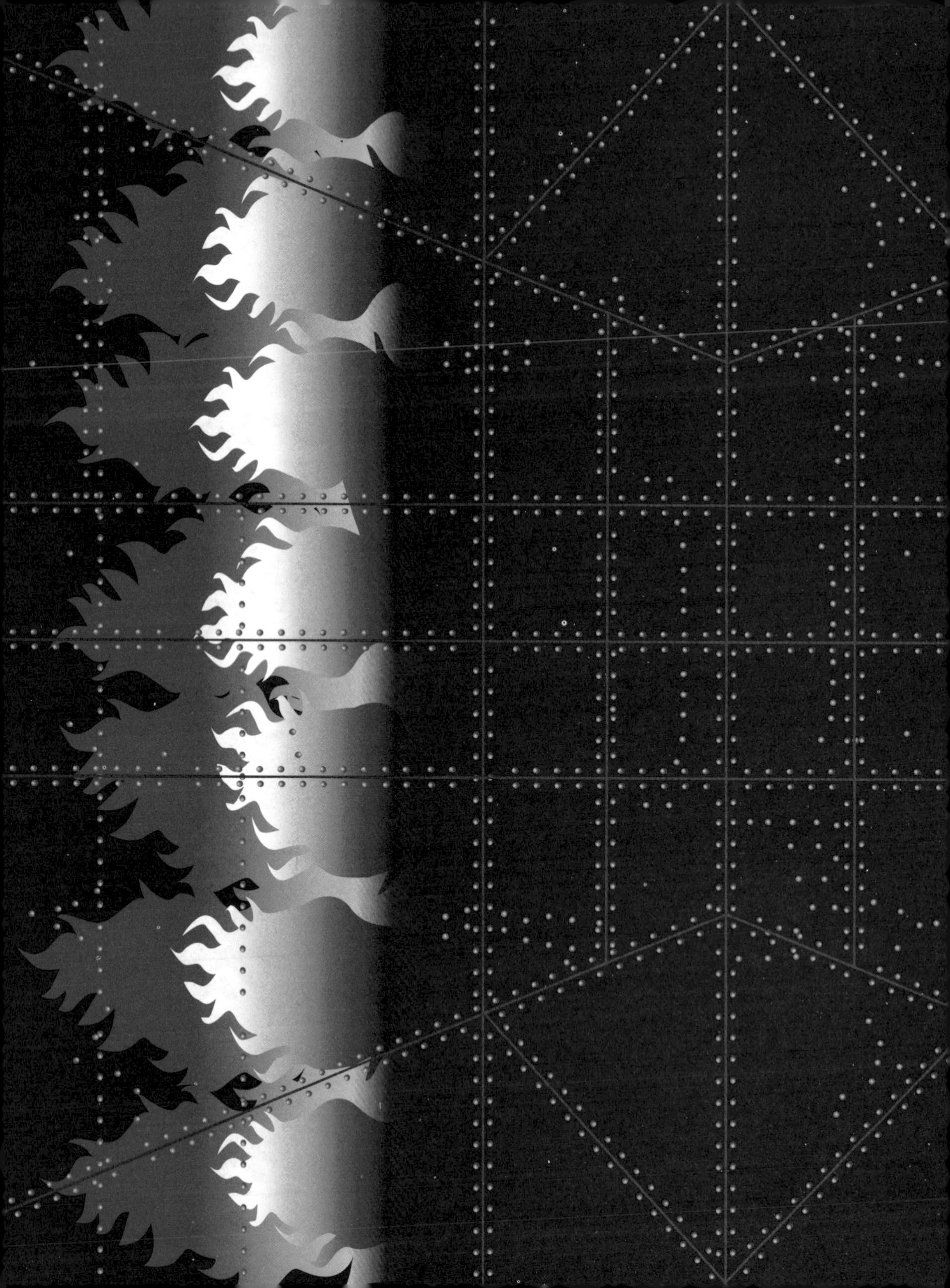

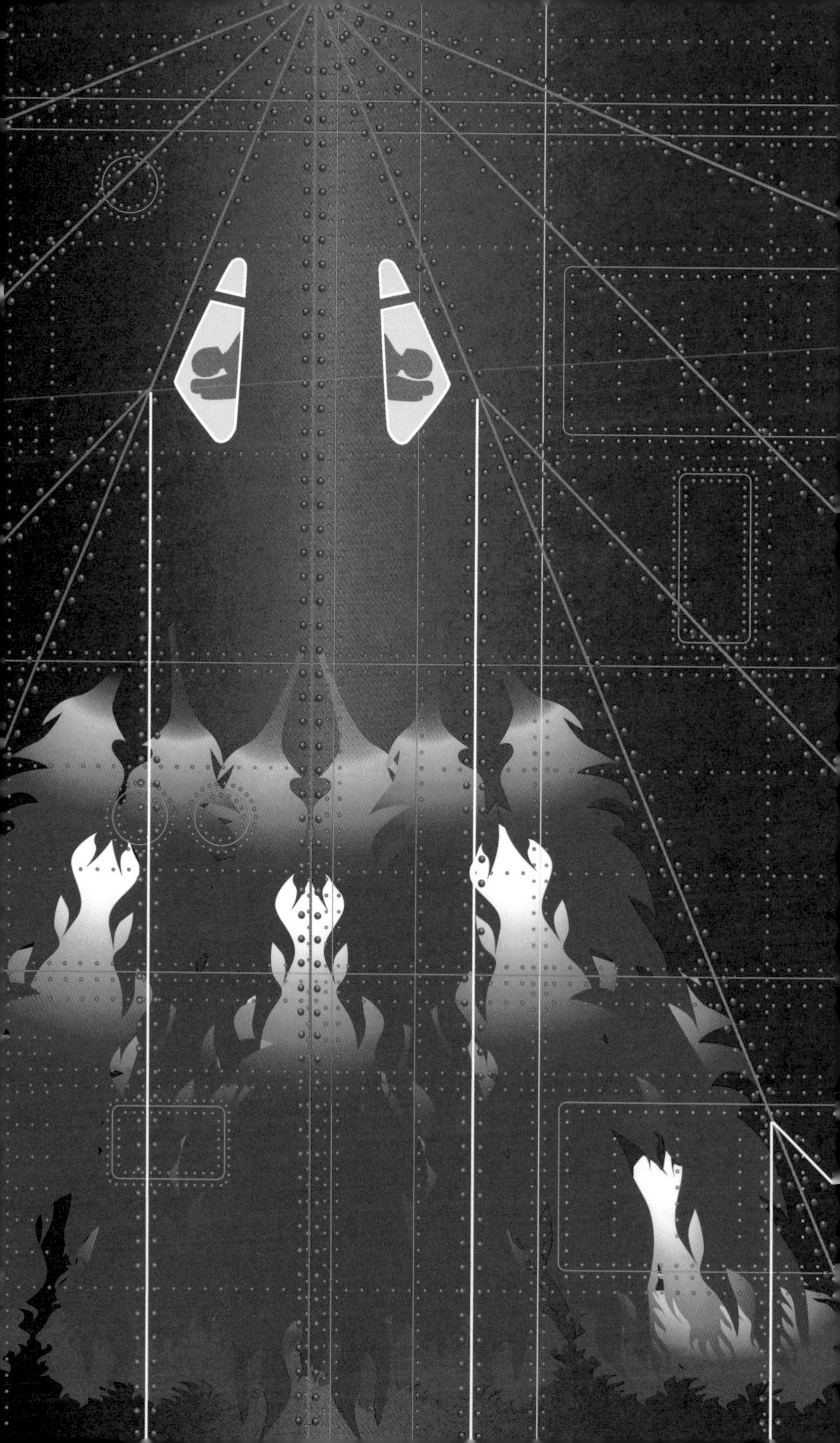

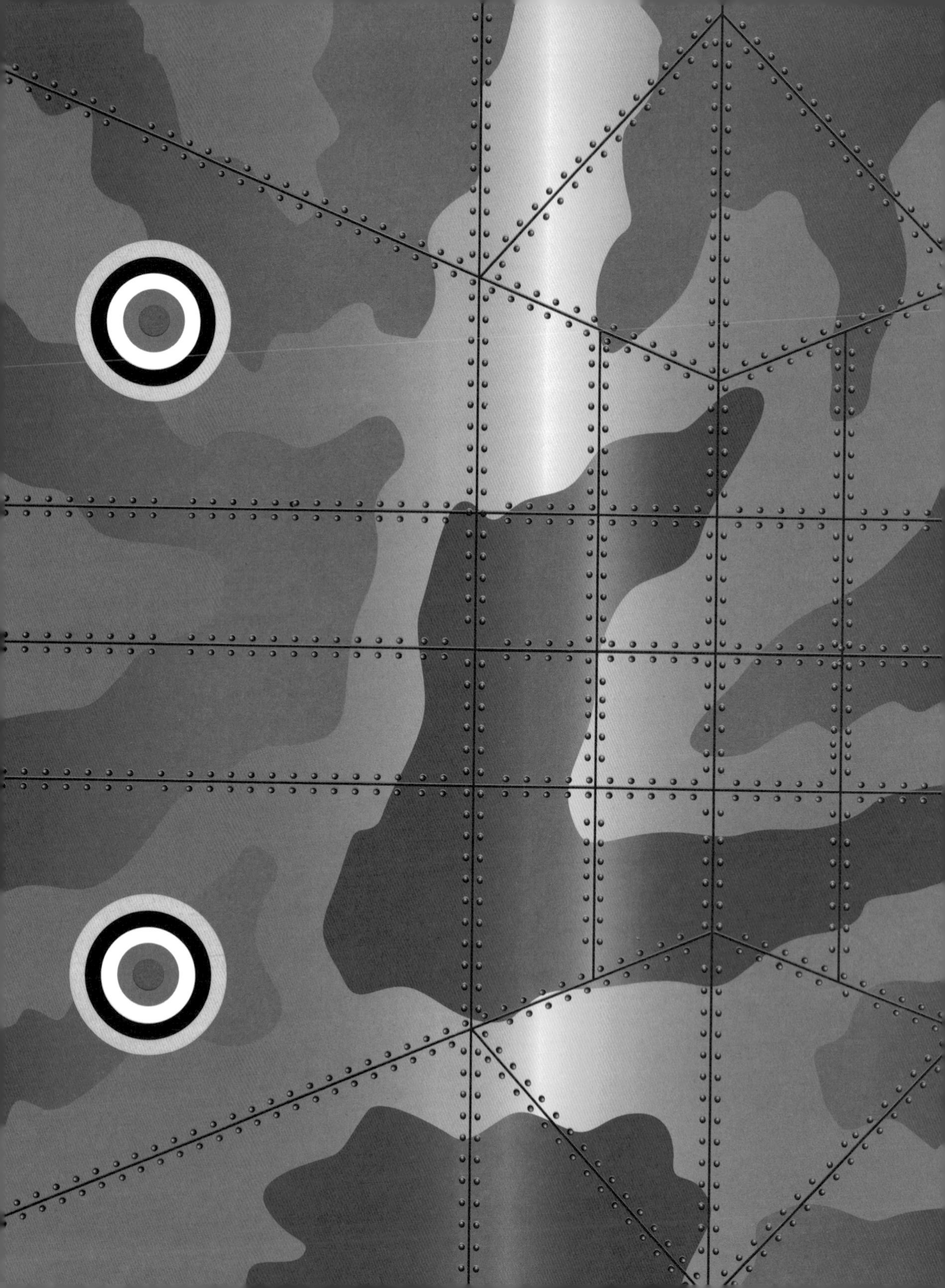

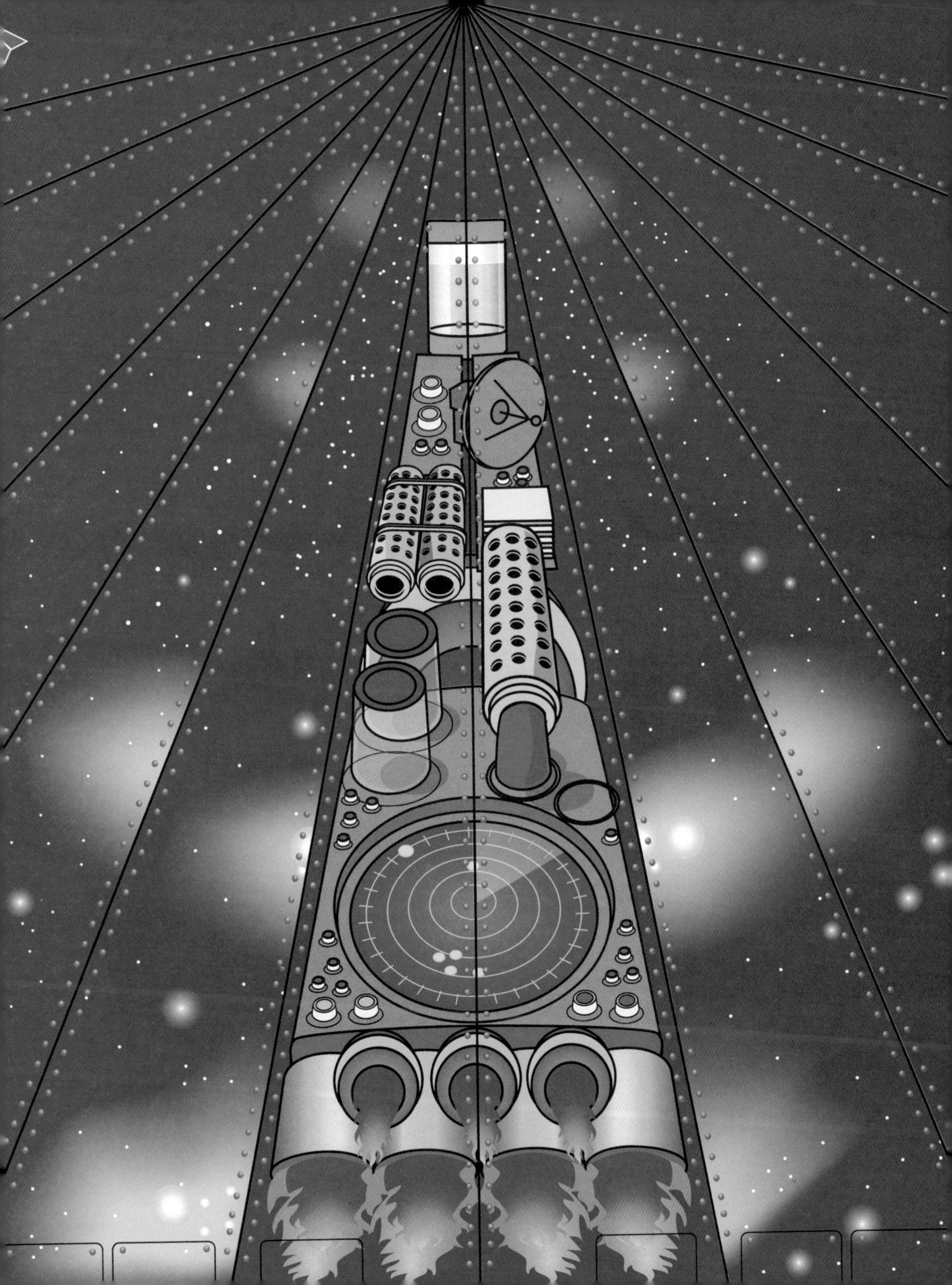

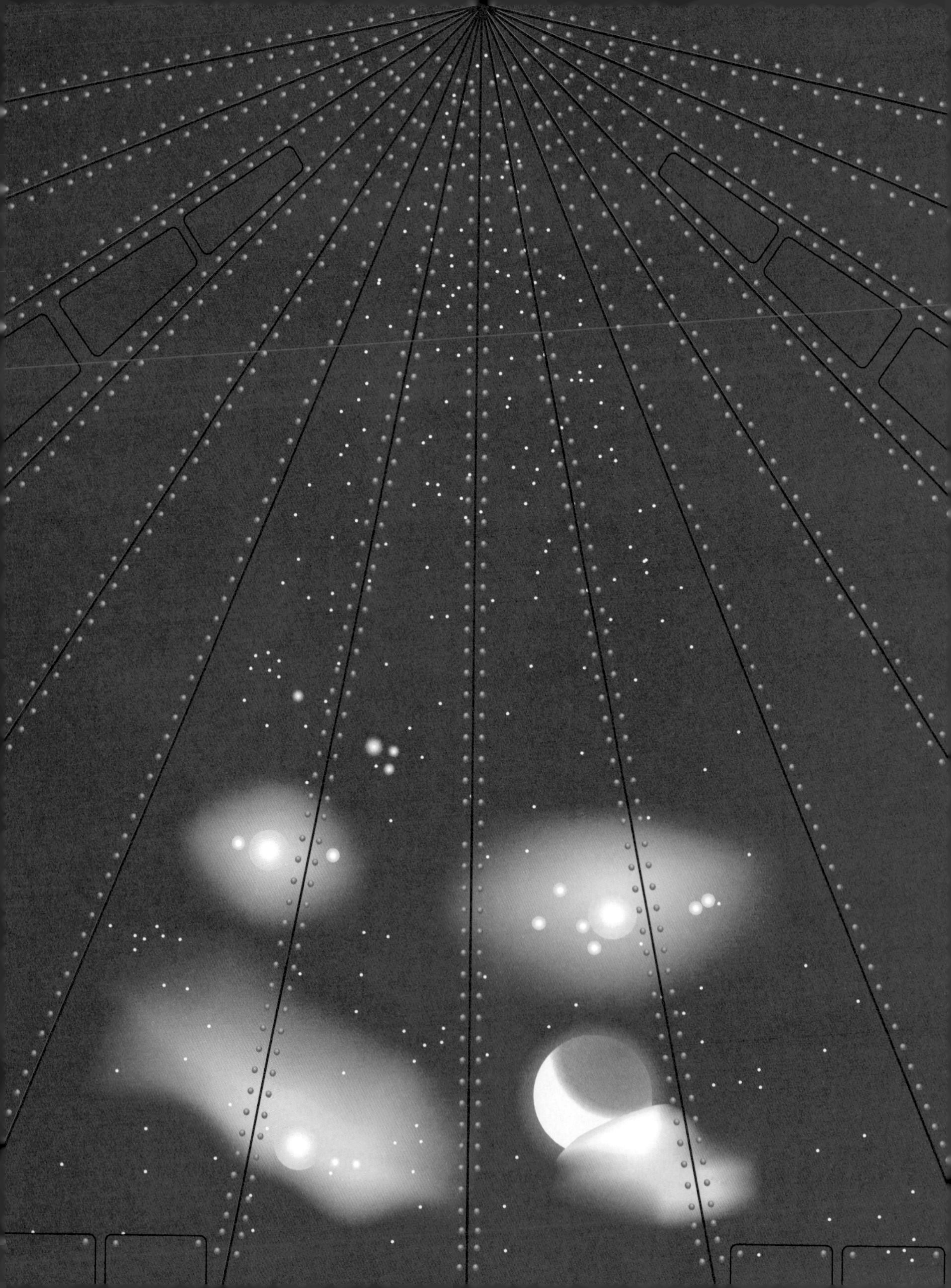

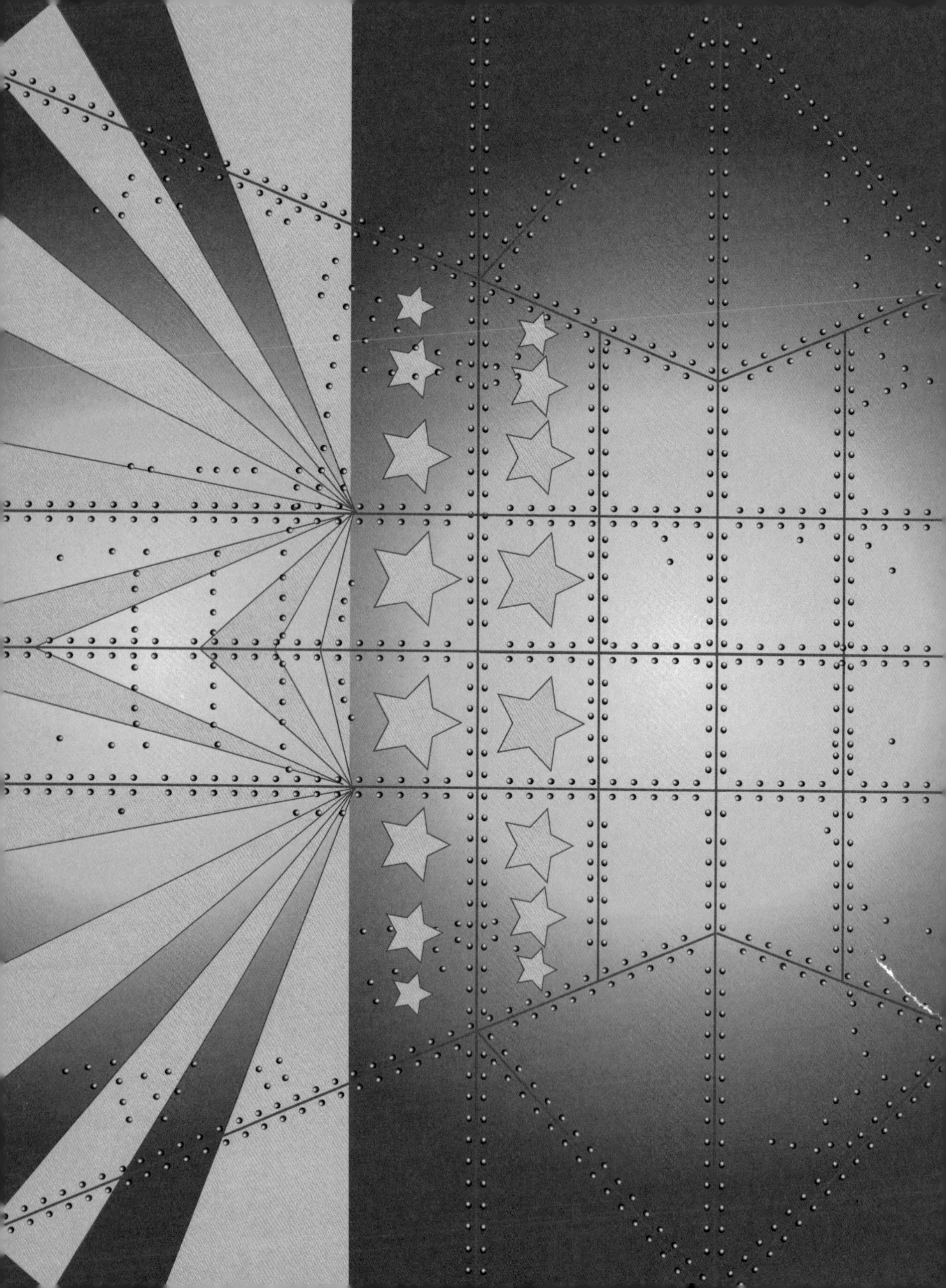

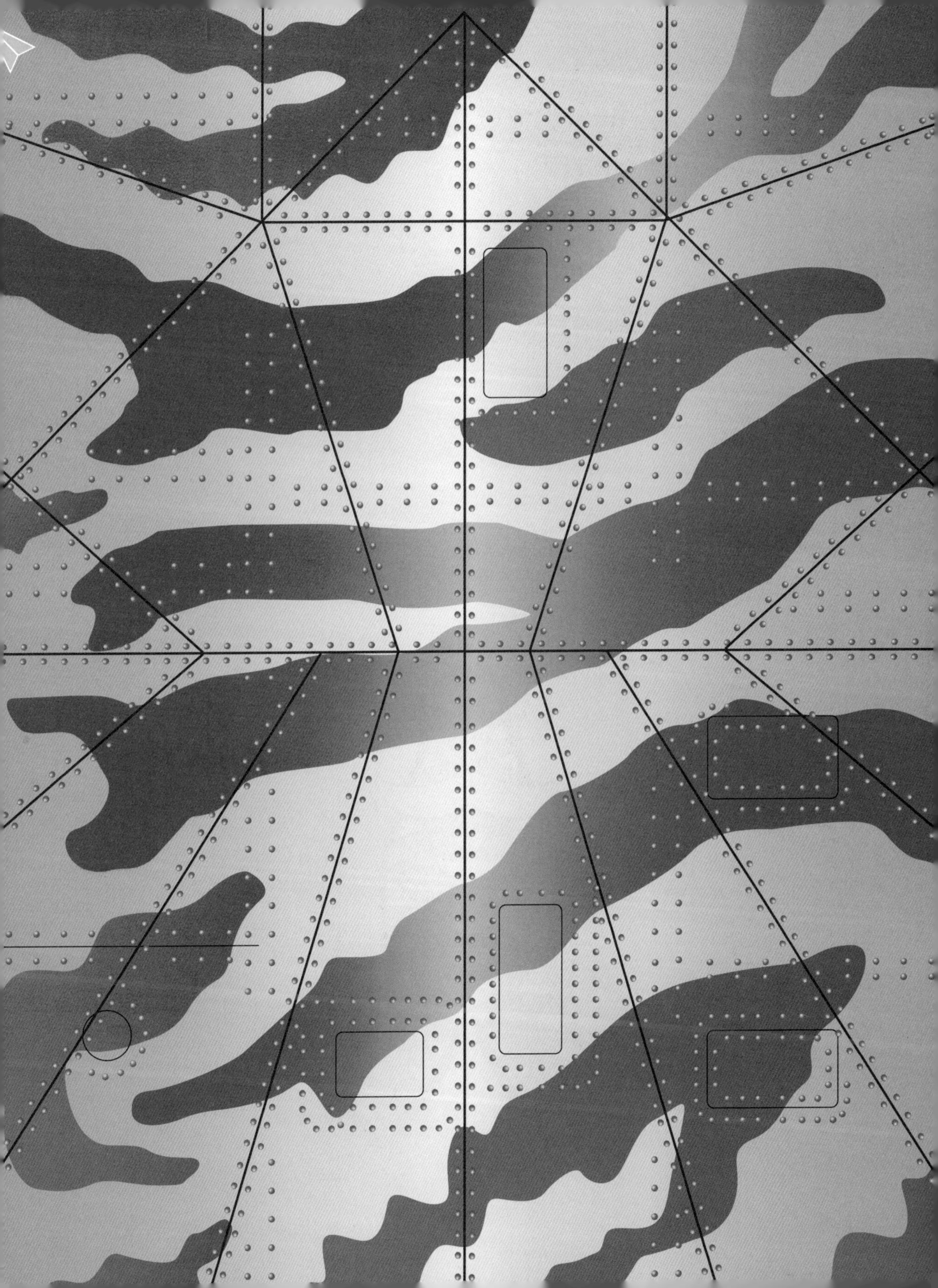

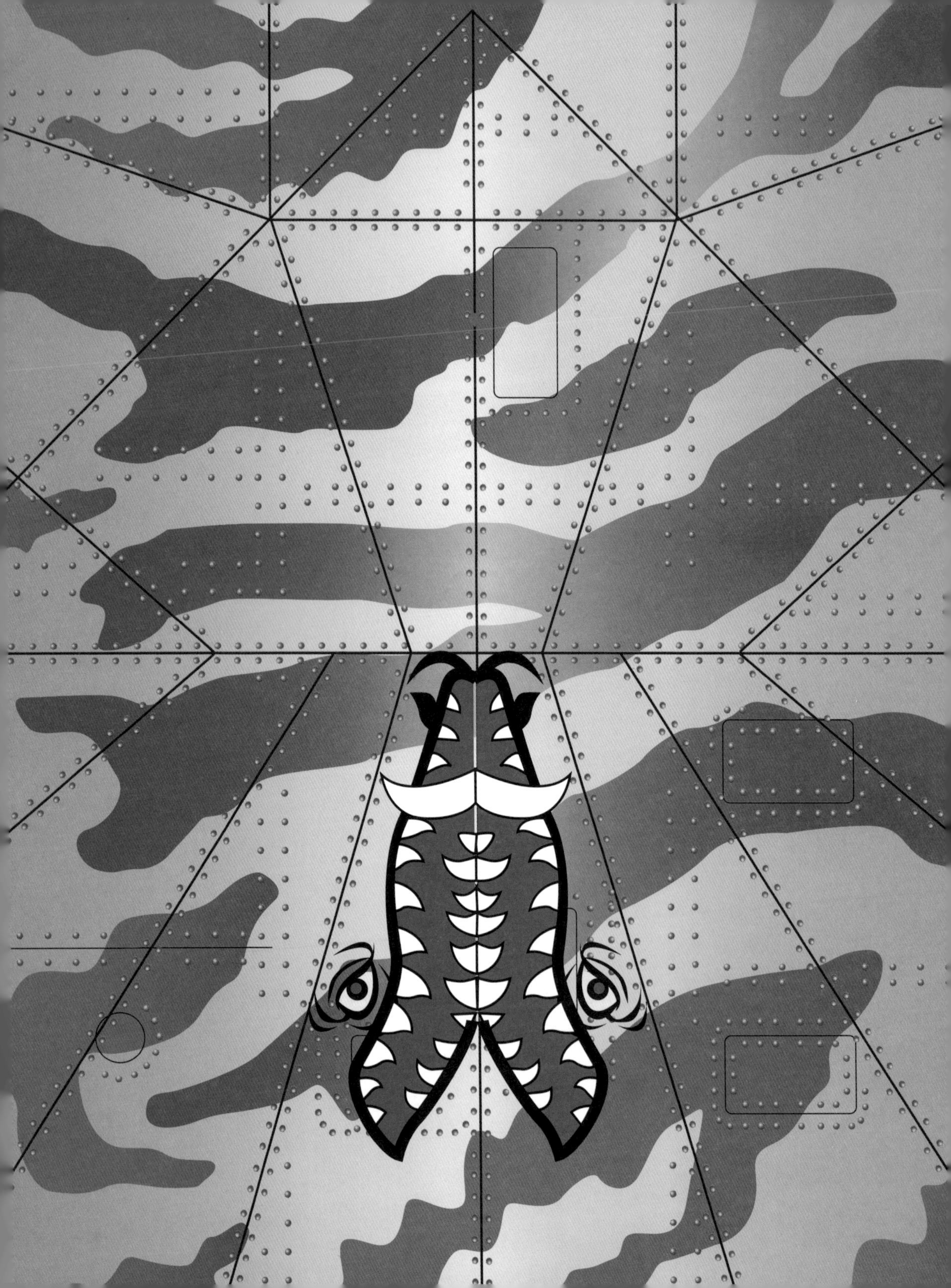

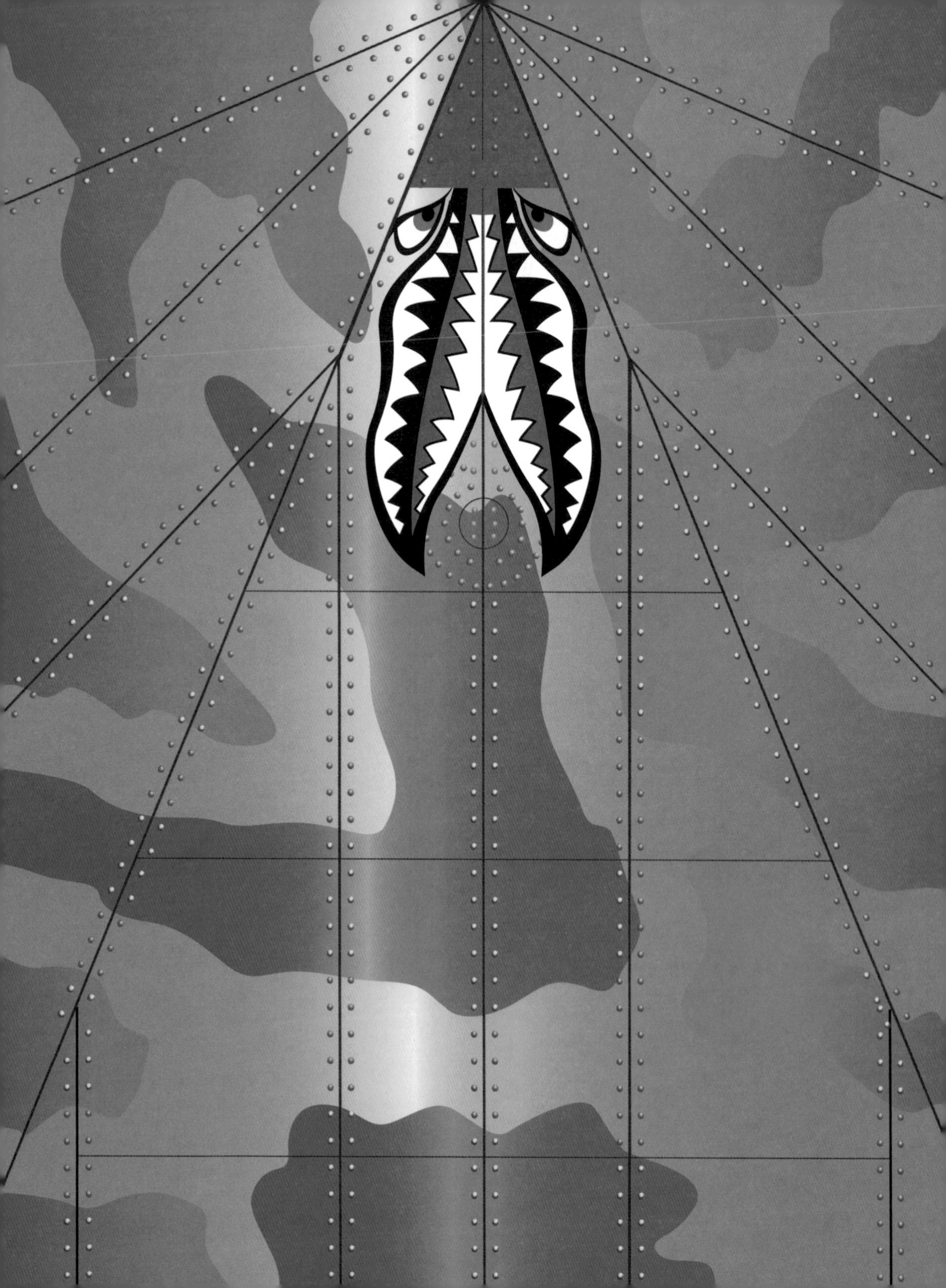

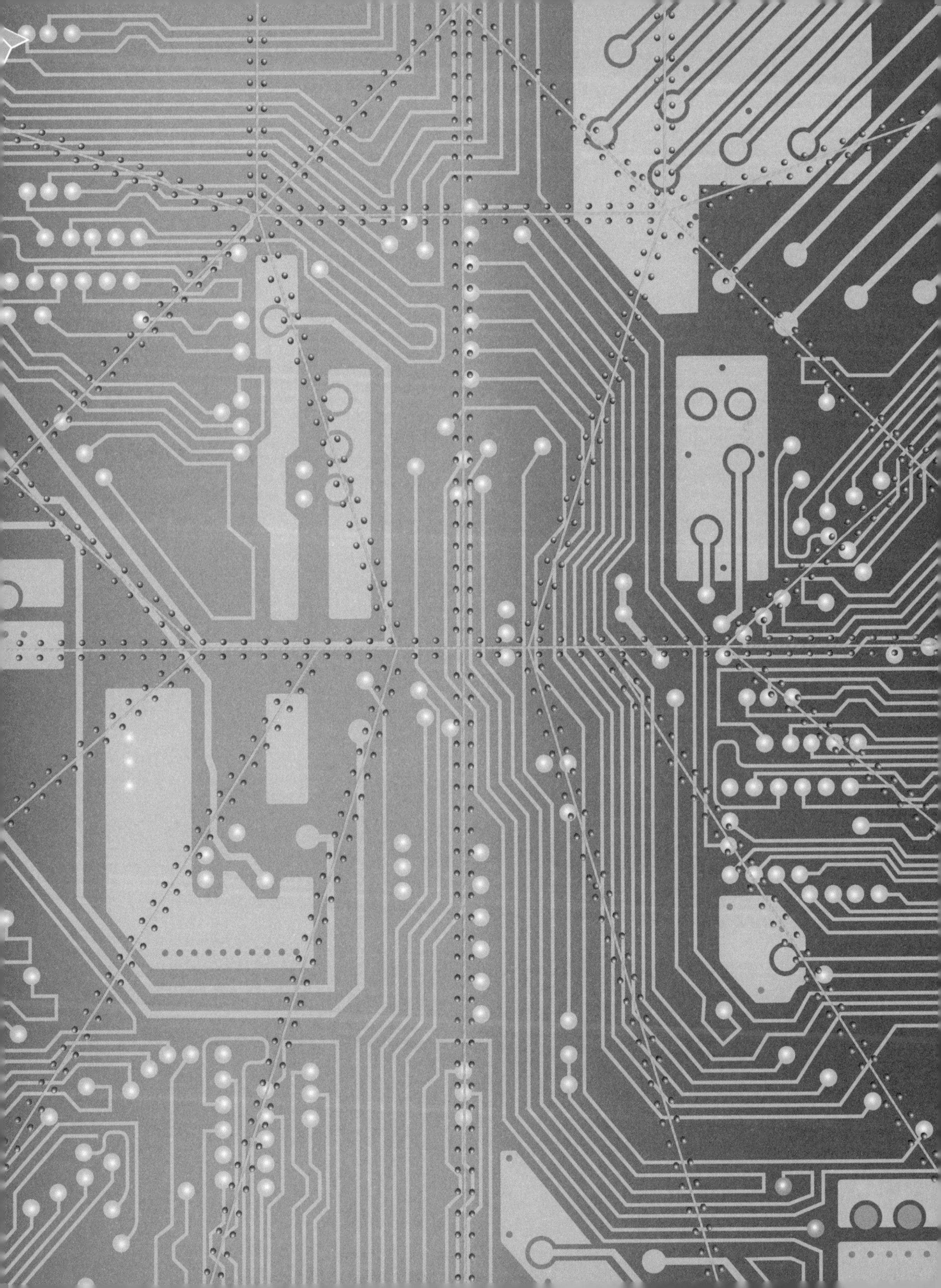

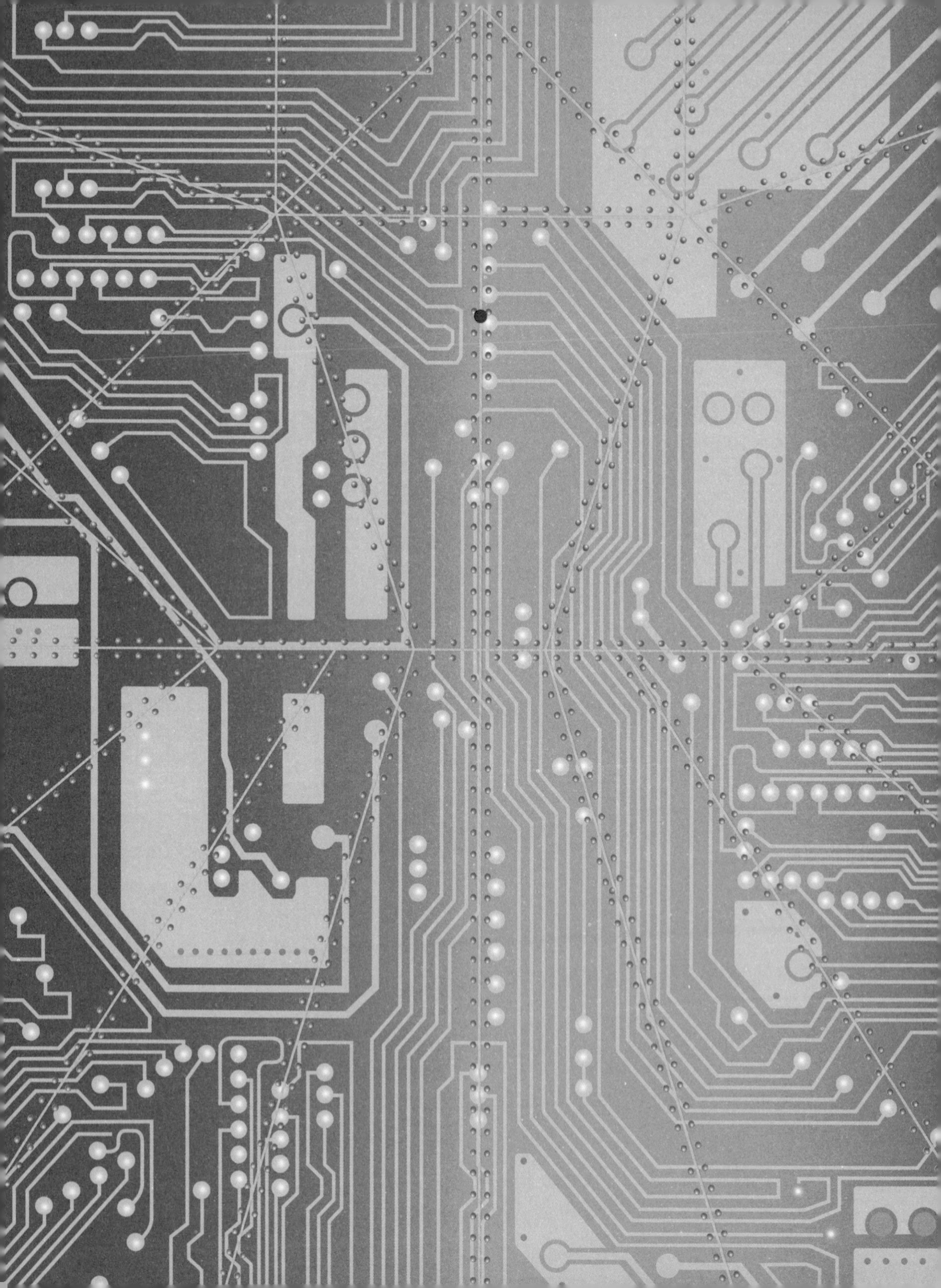

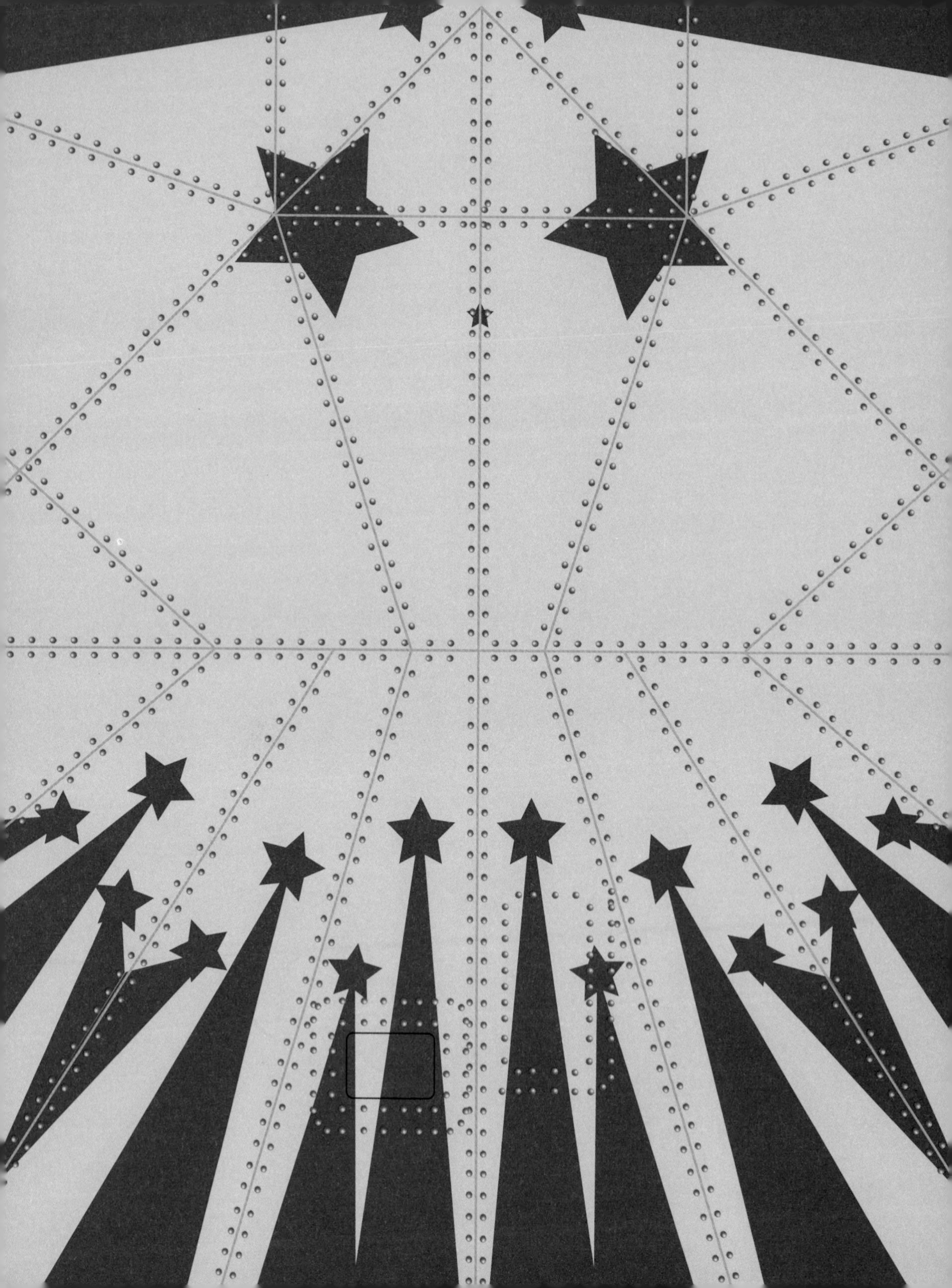

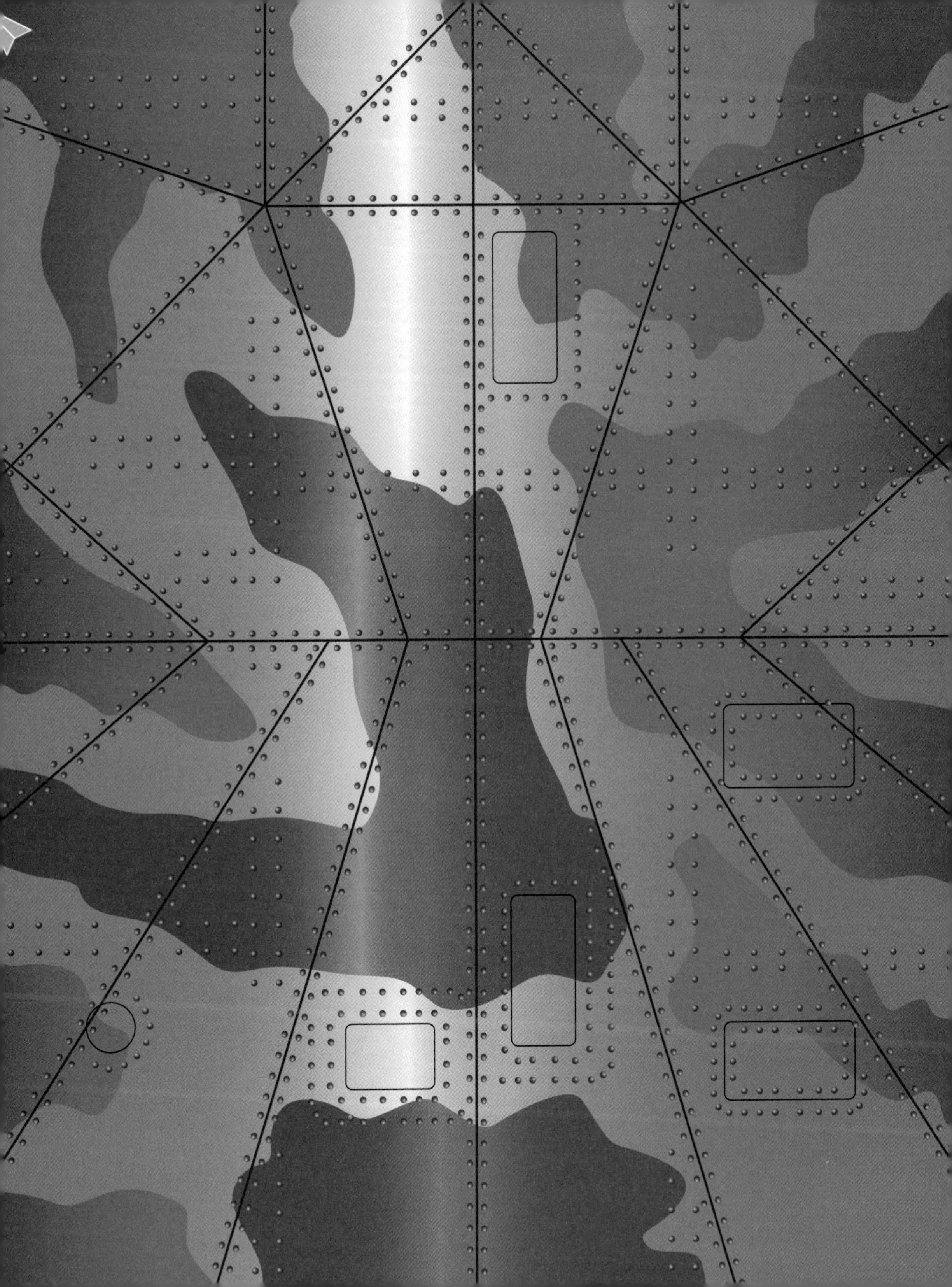

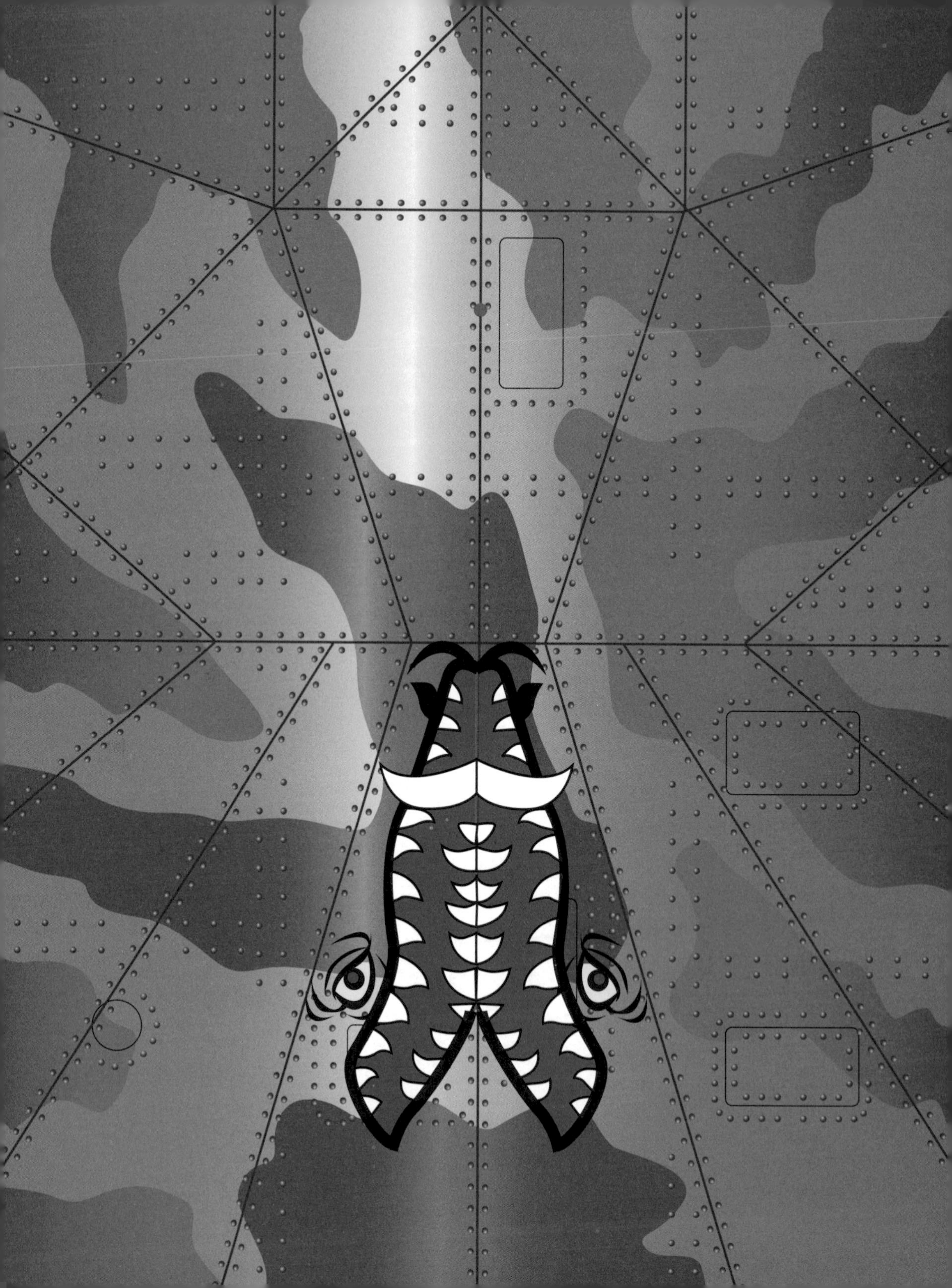

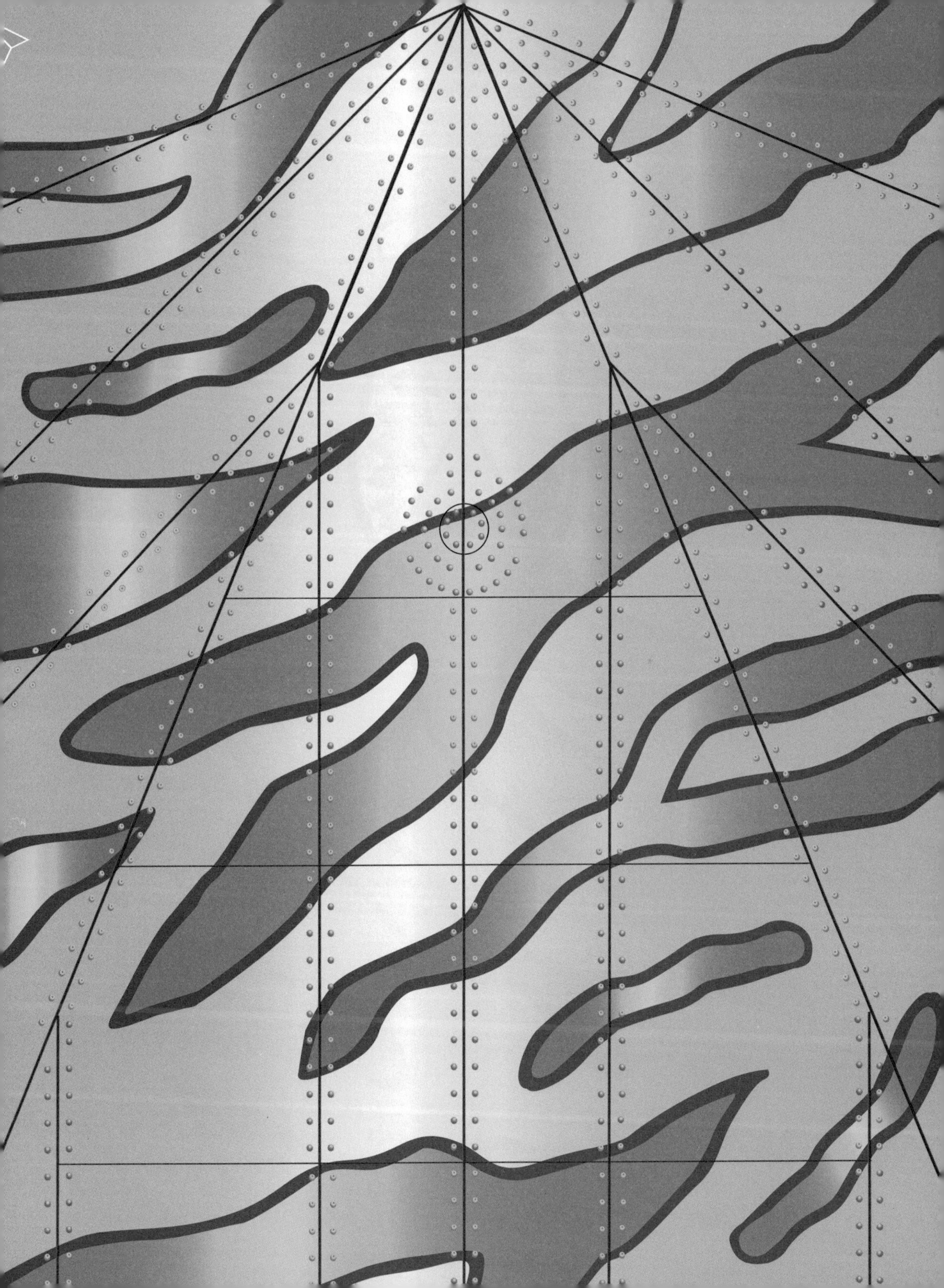

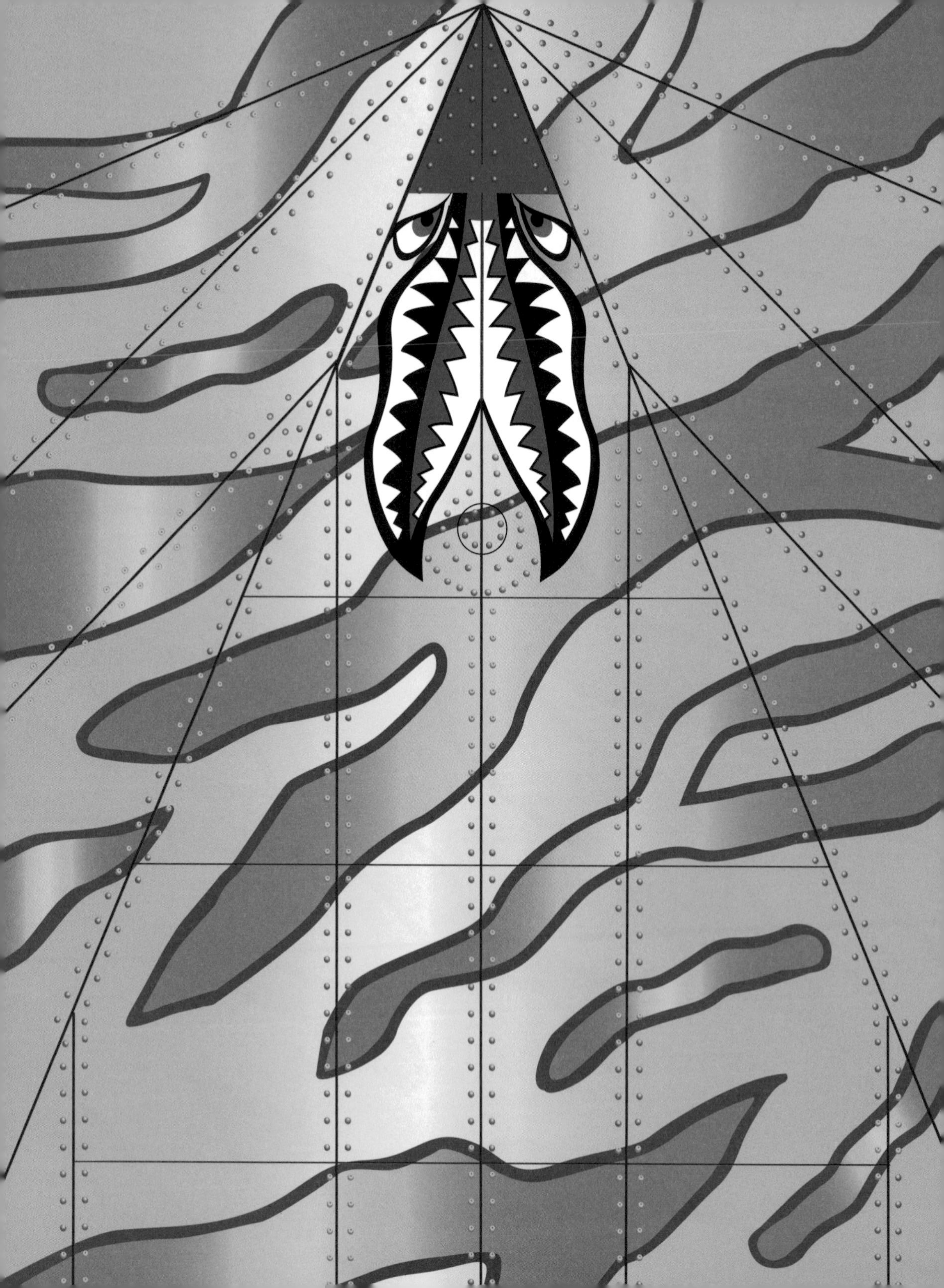

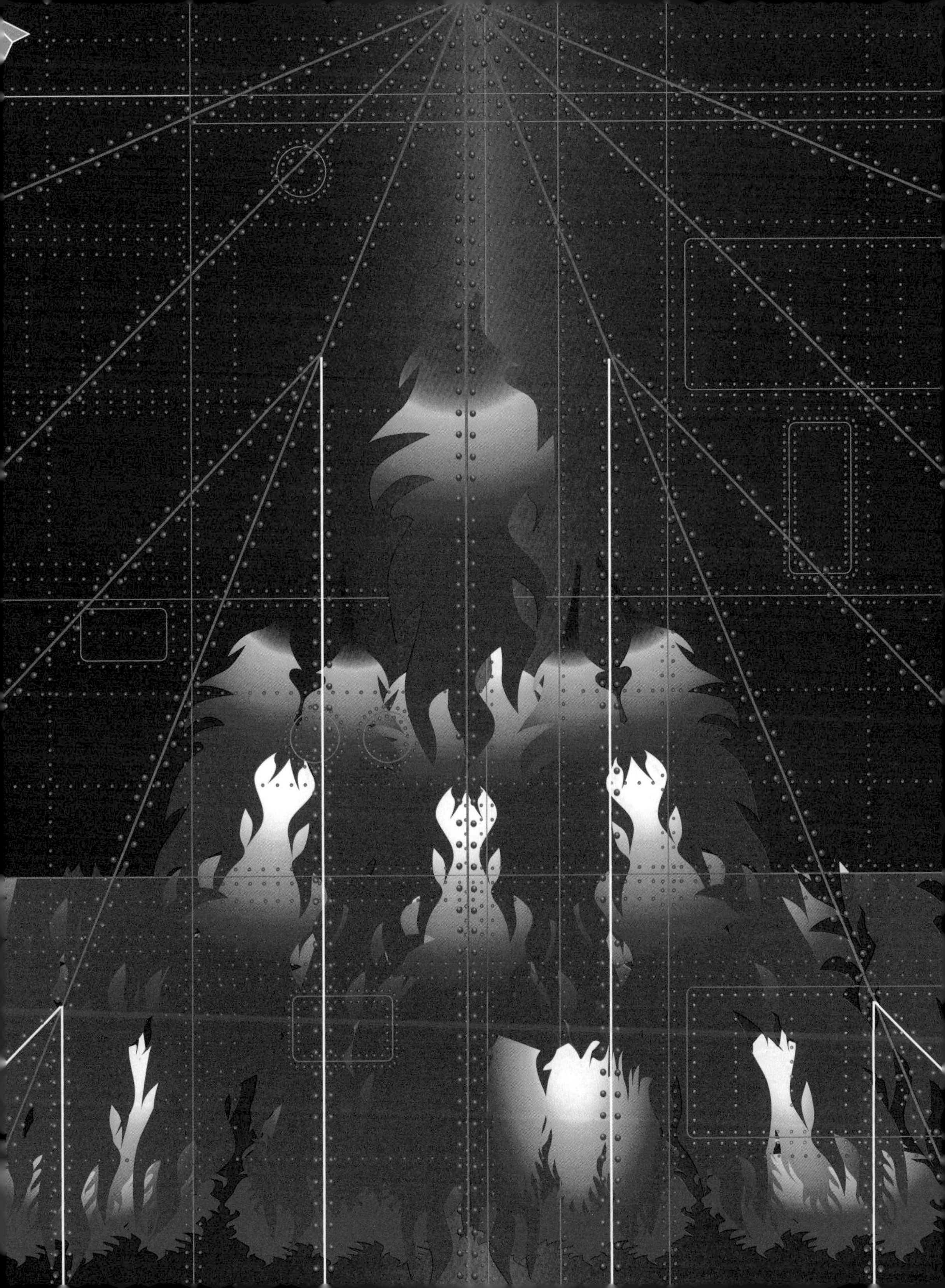

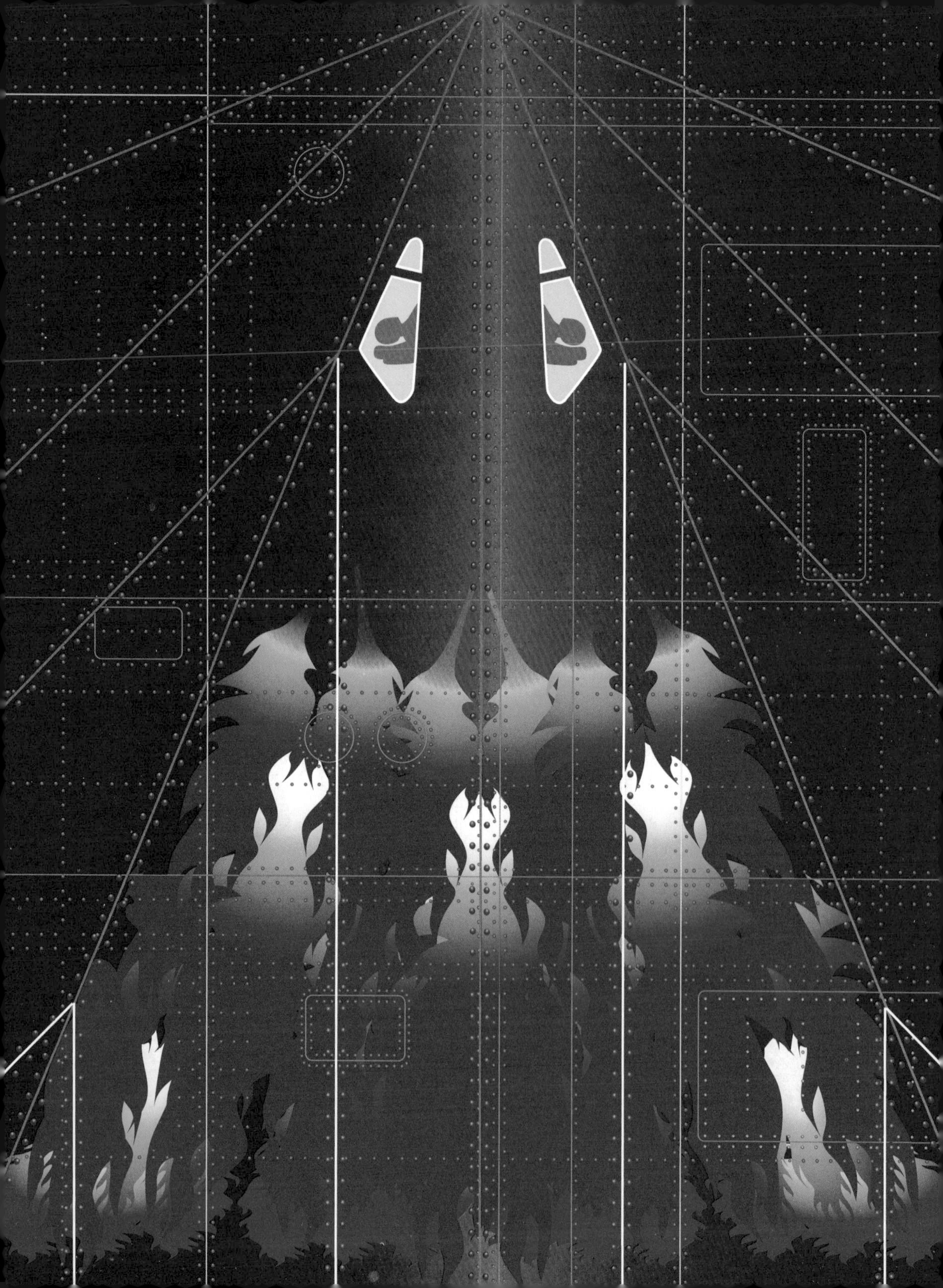

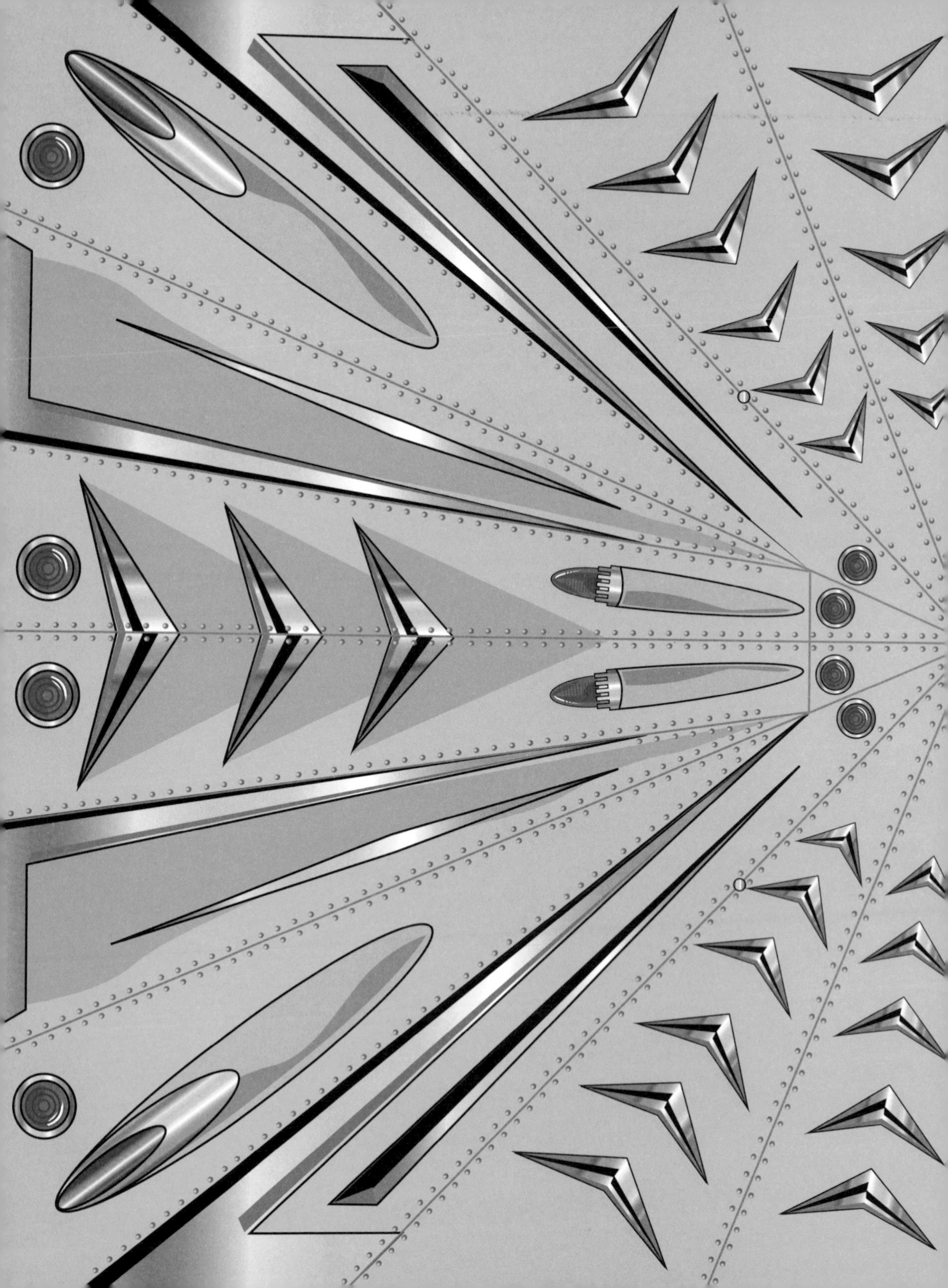

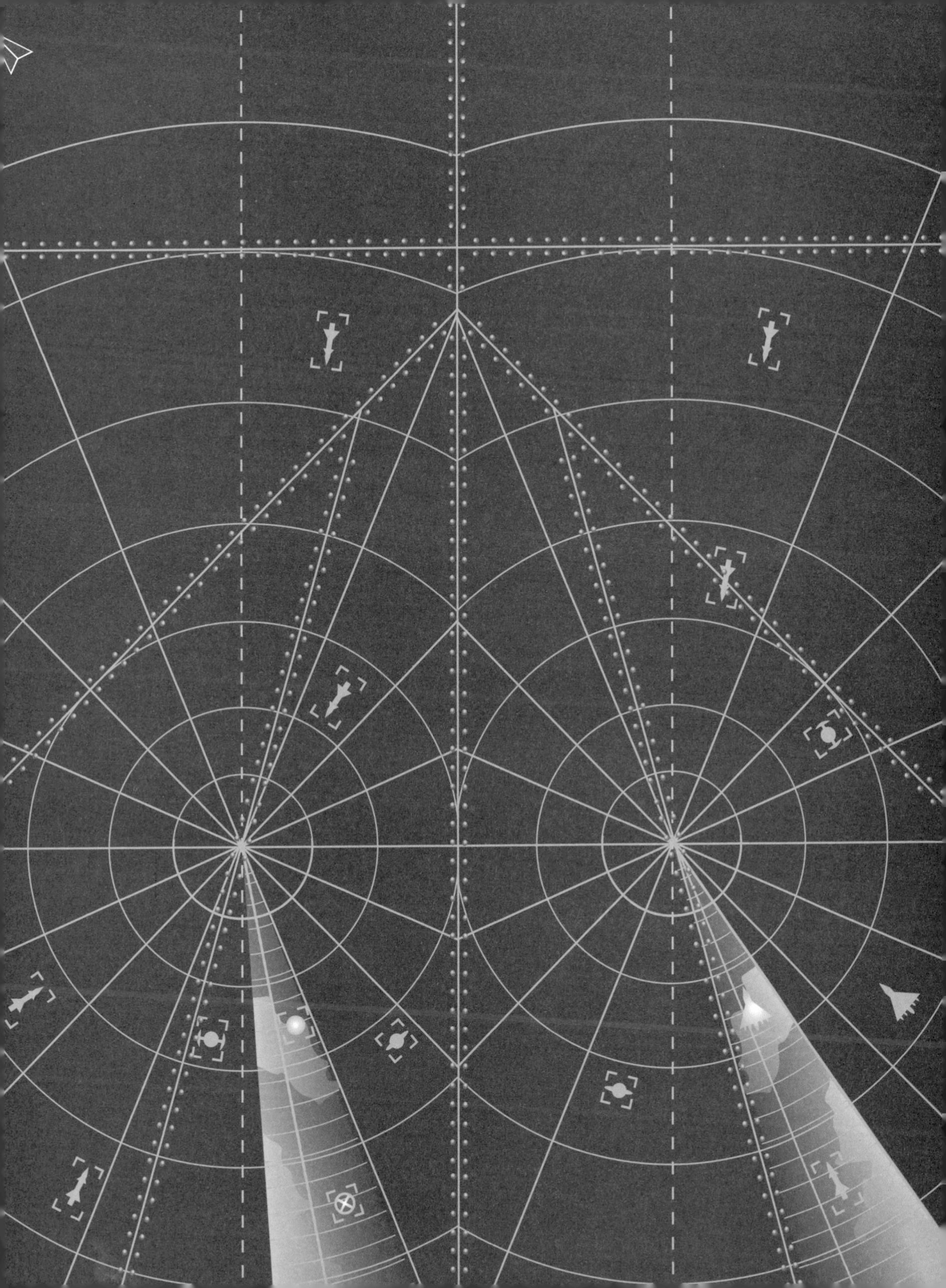

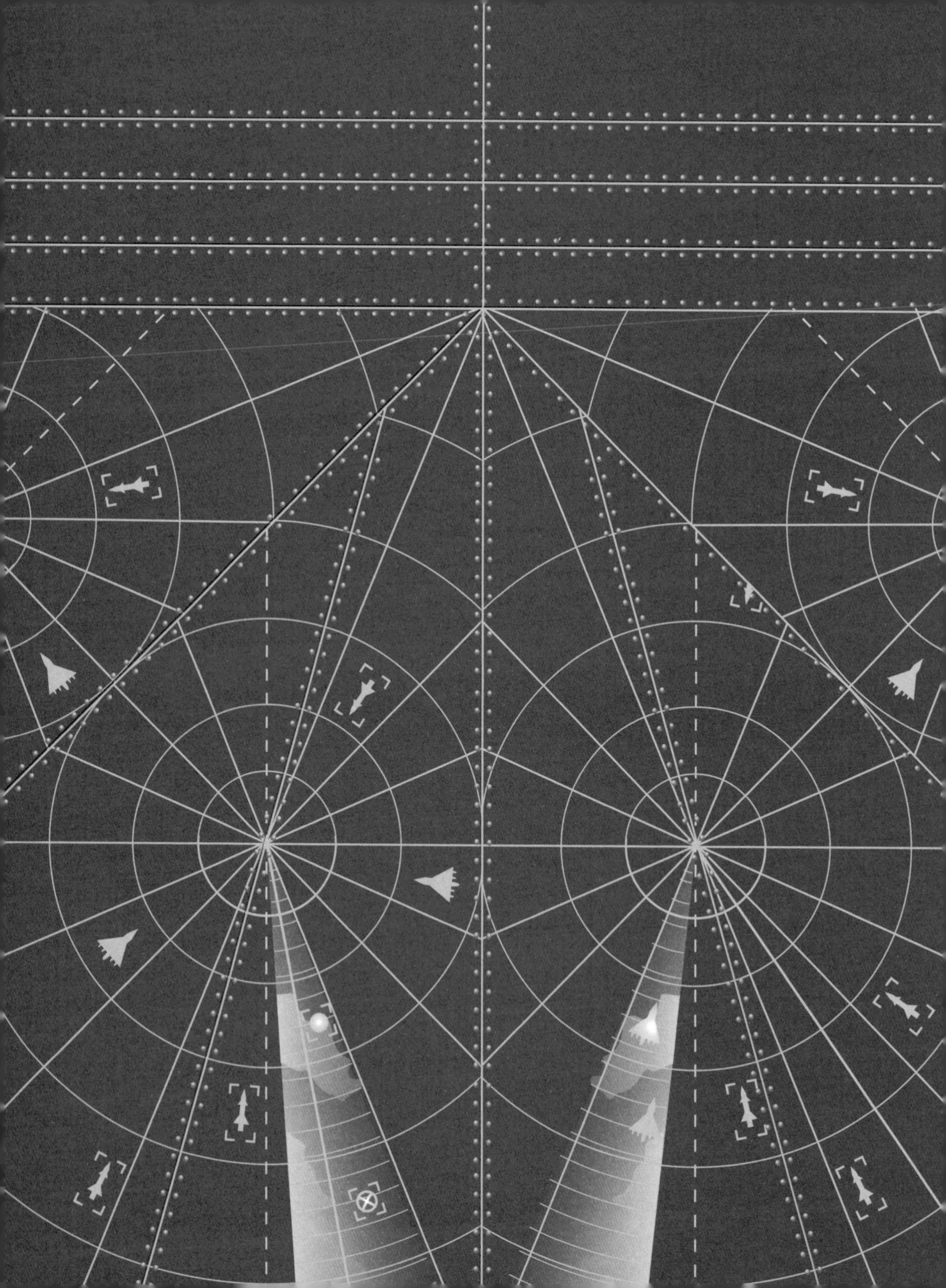

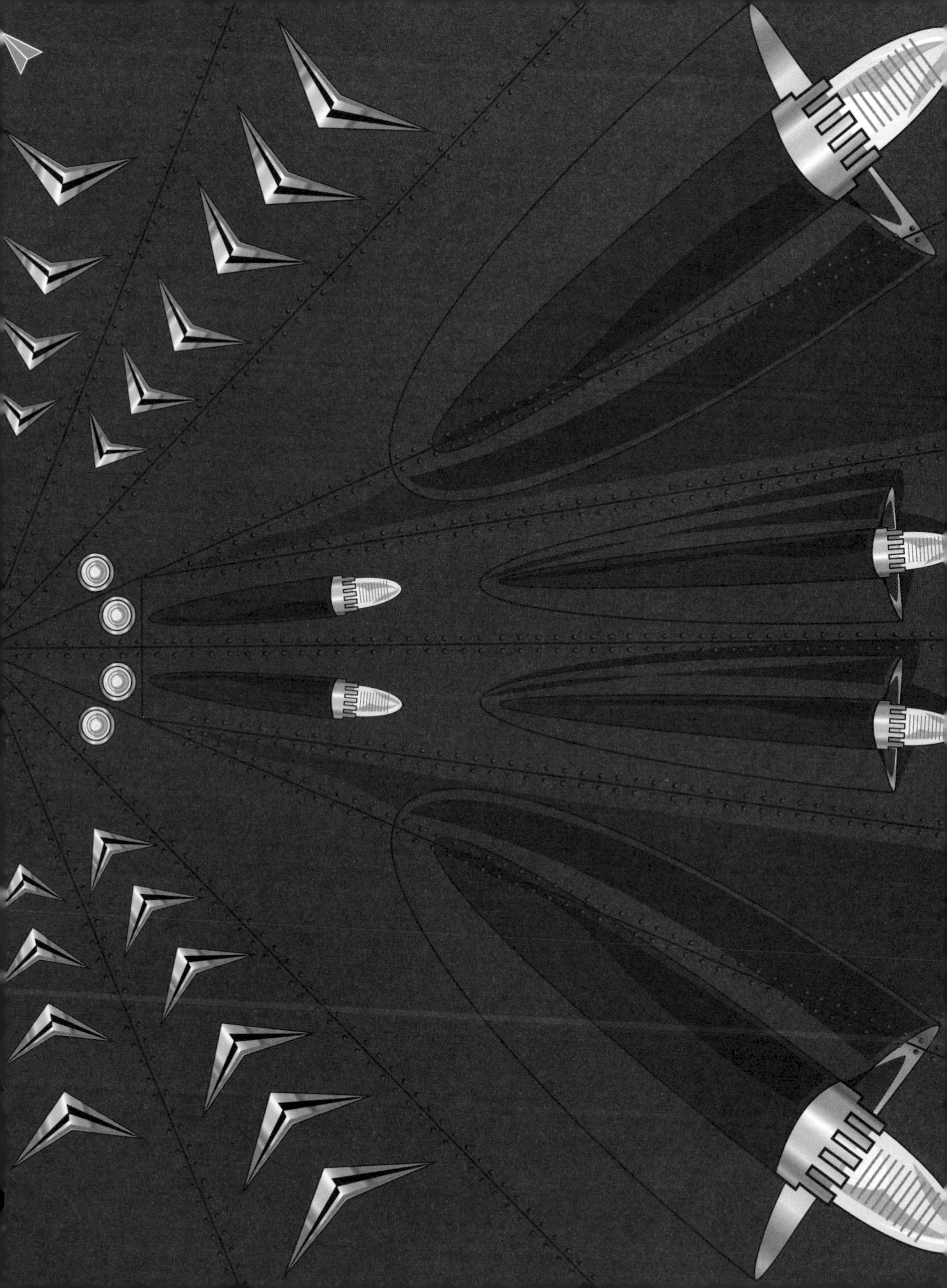

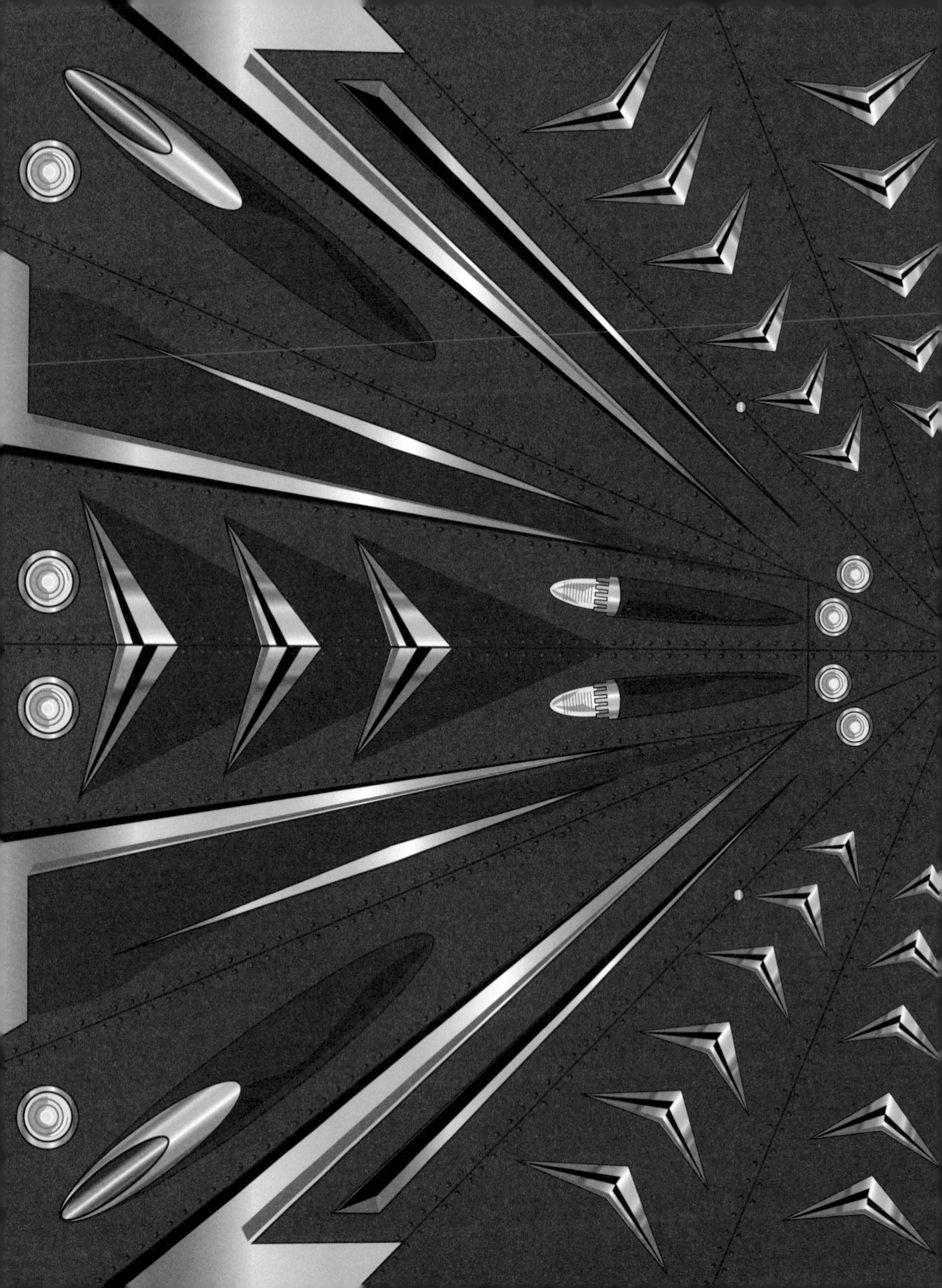

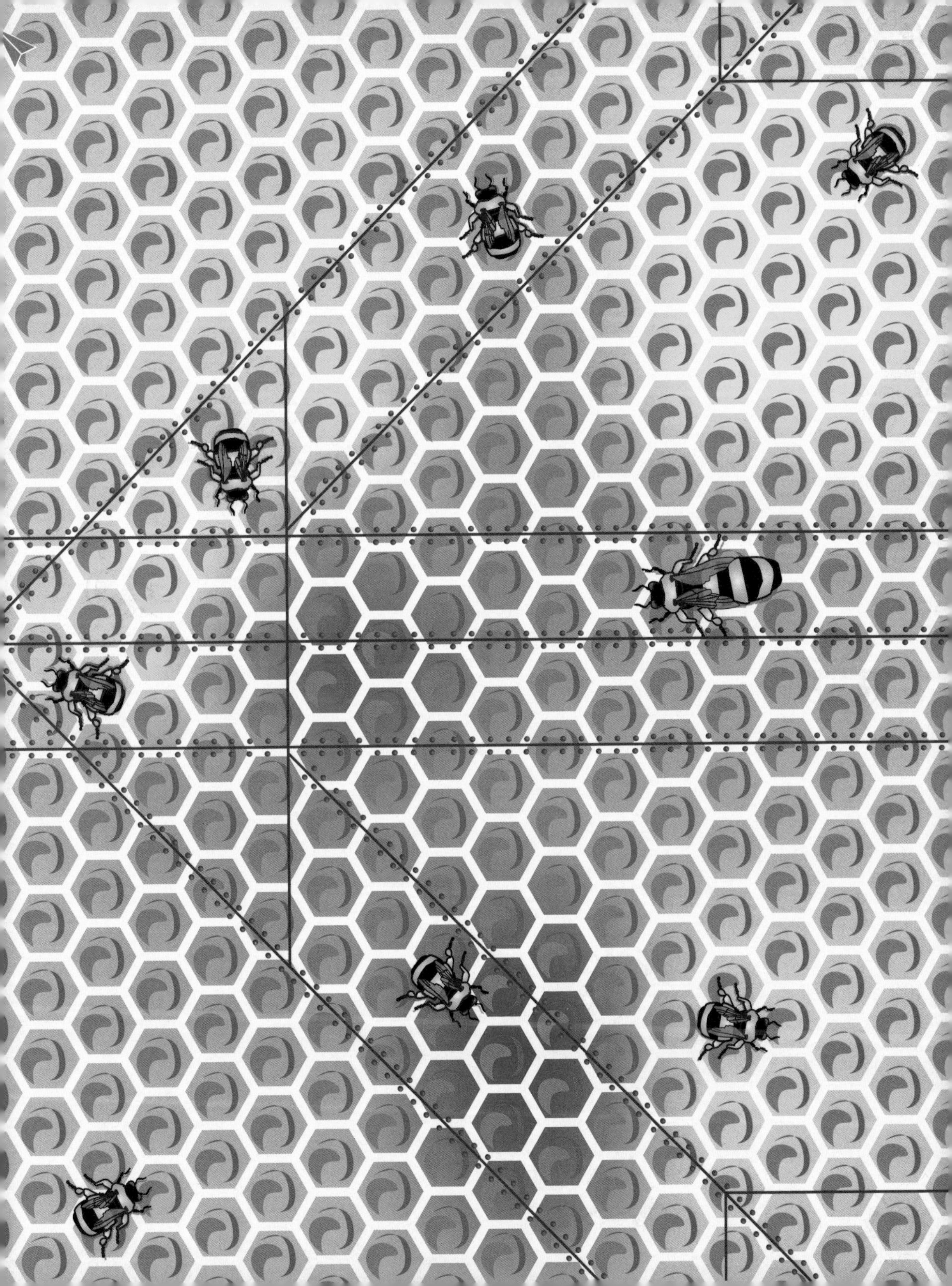

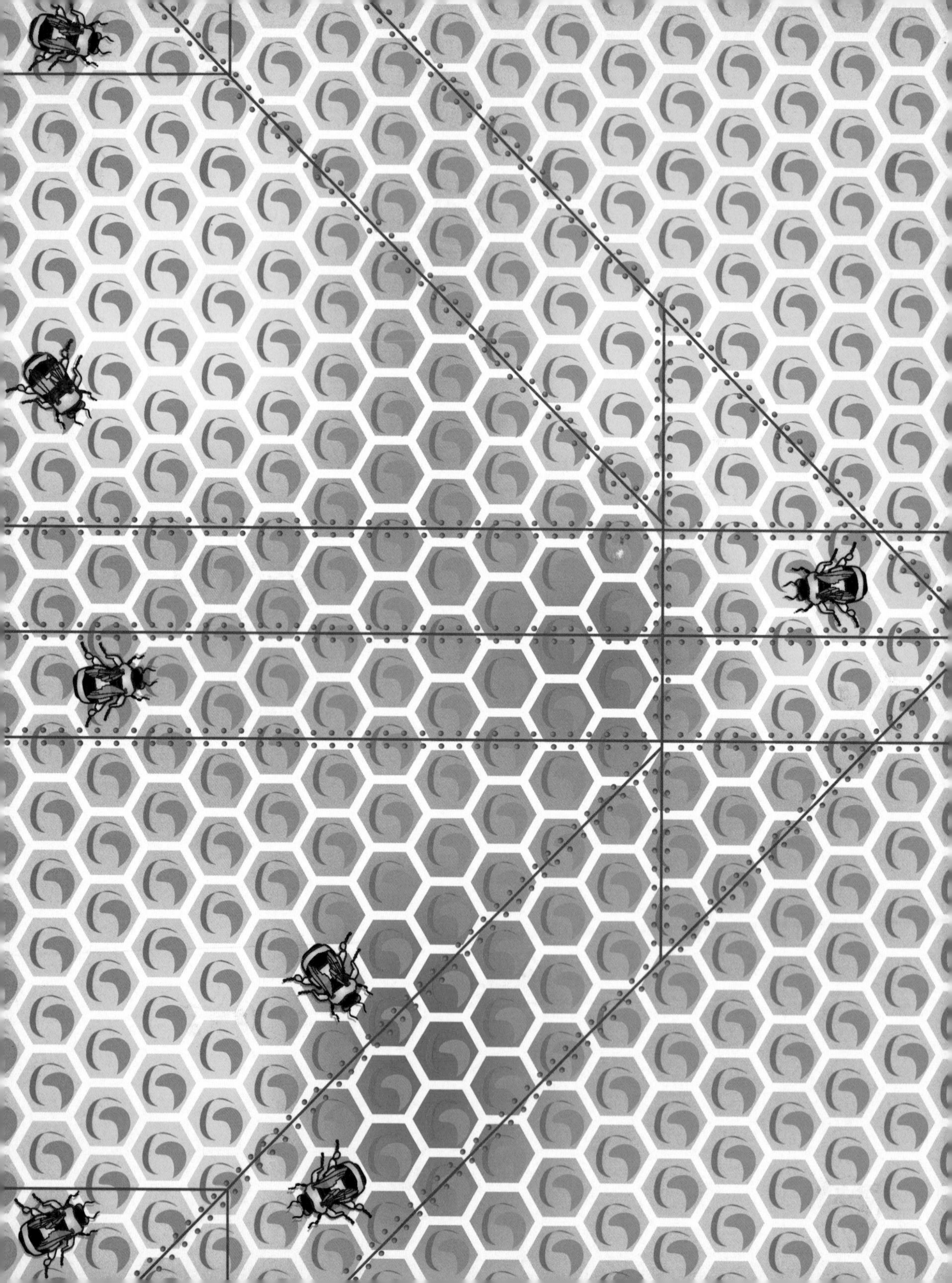

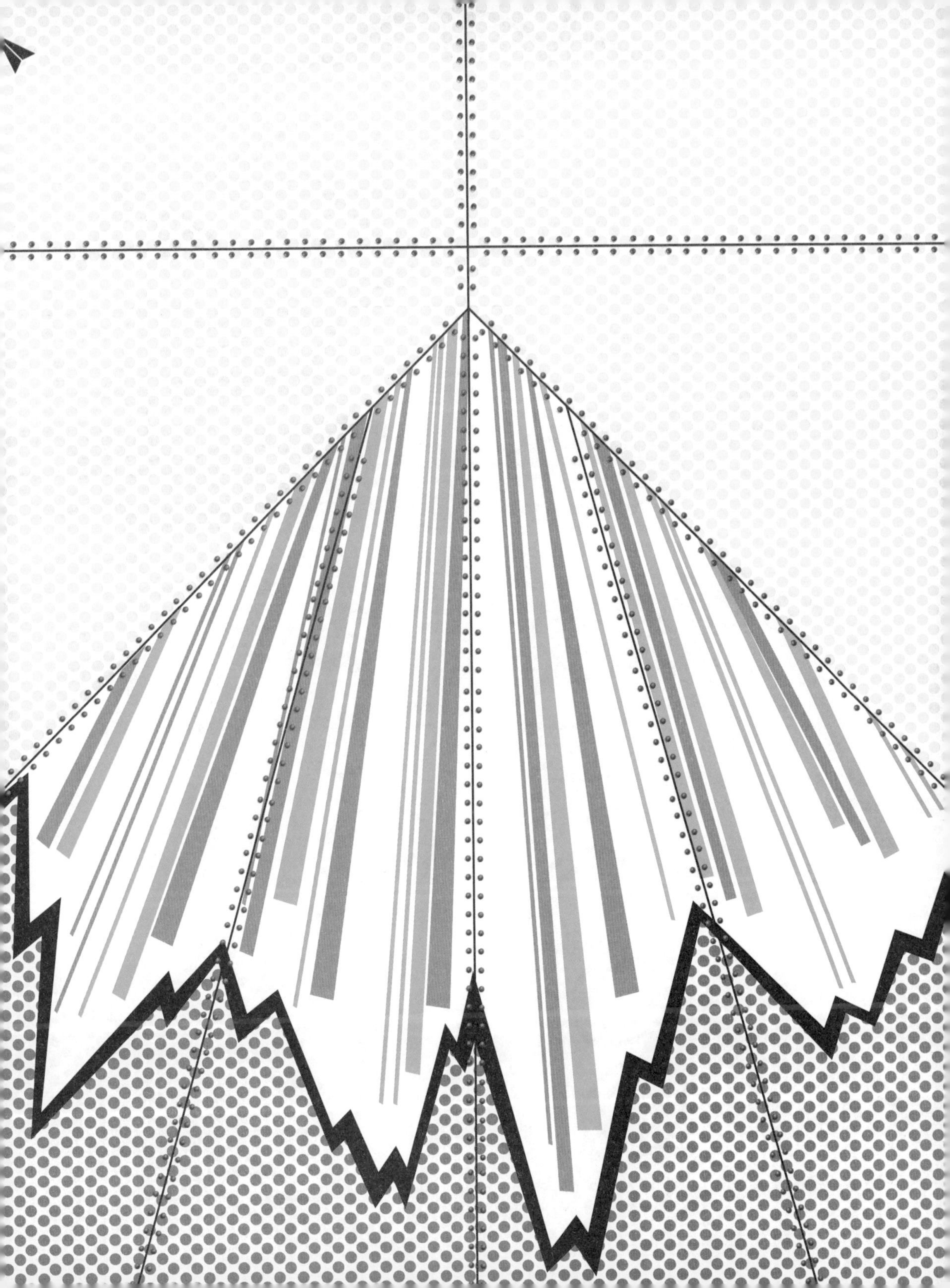

ZOOOM
ZOOOM

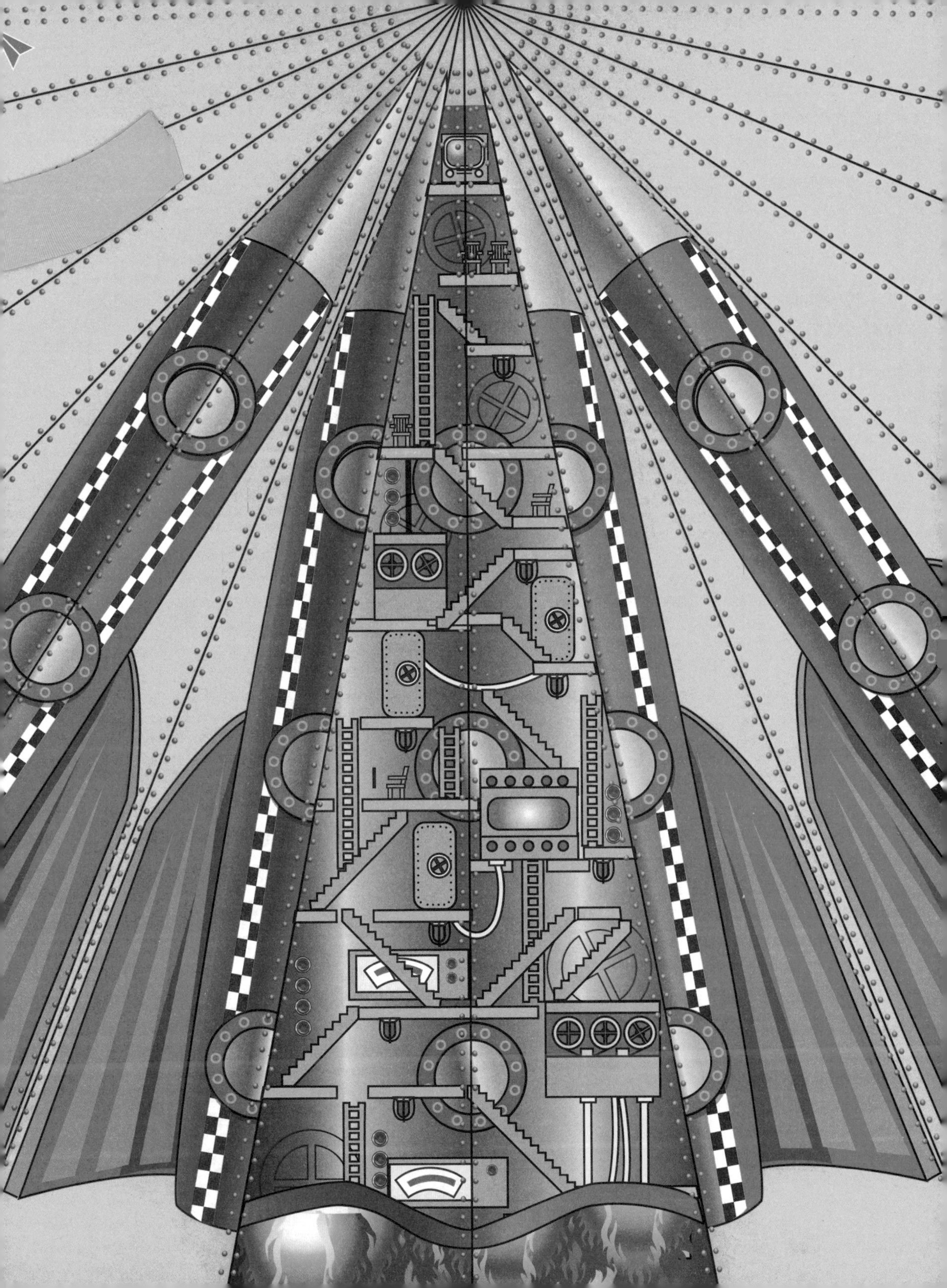

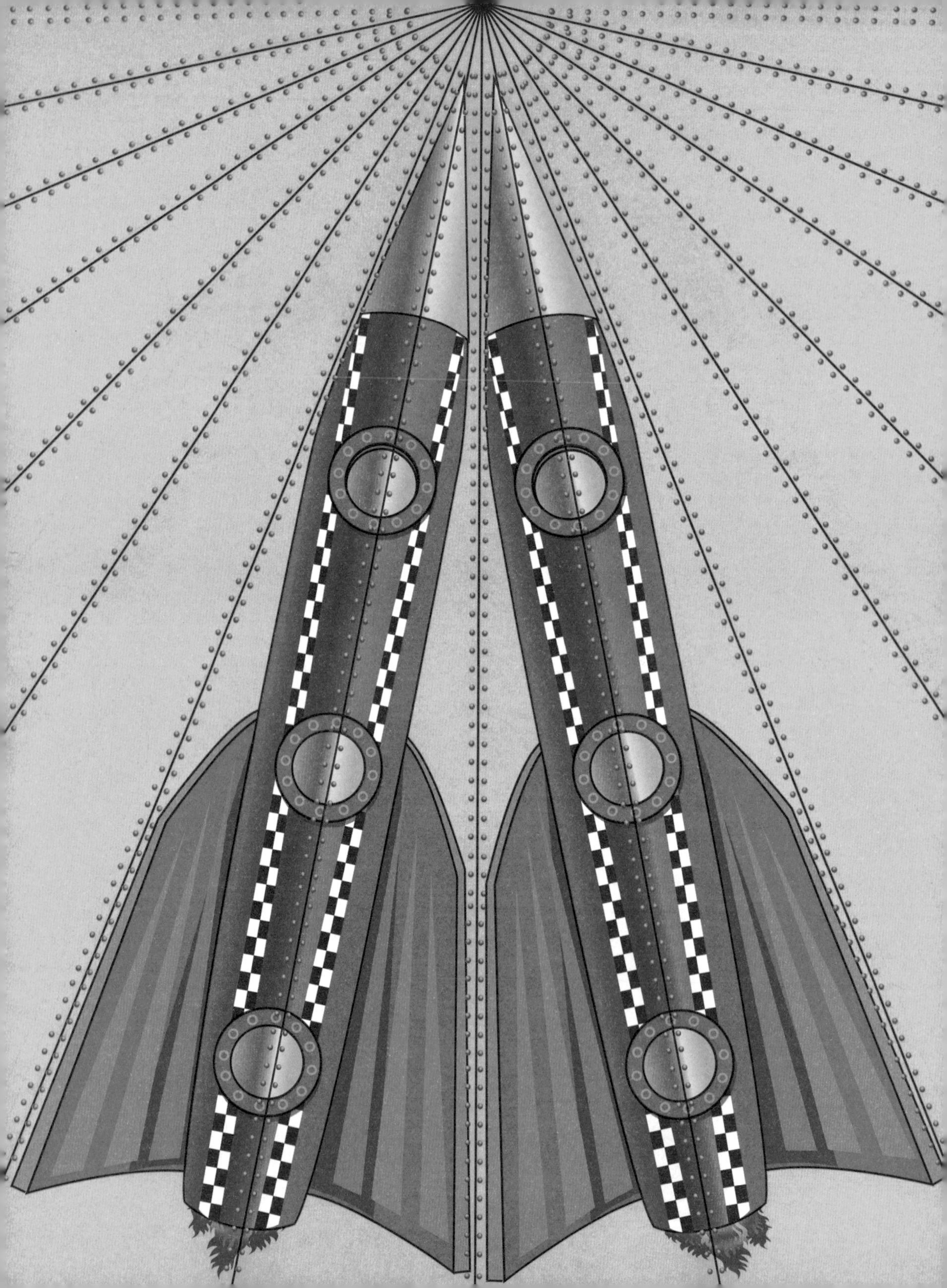

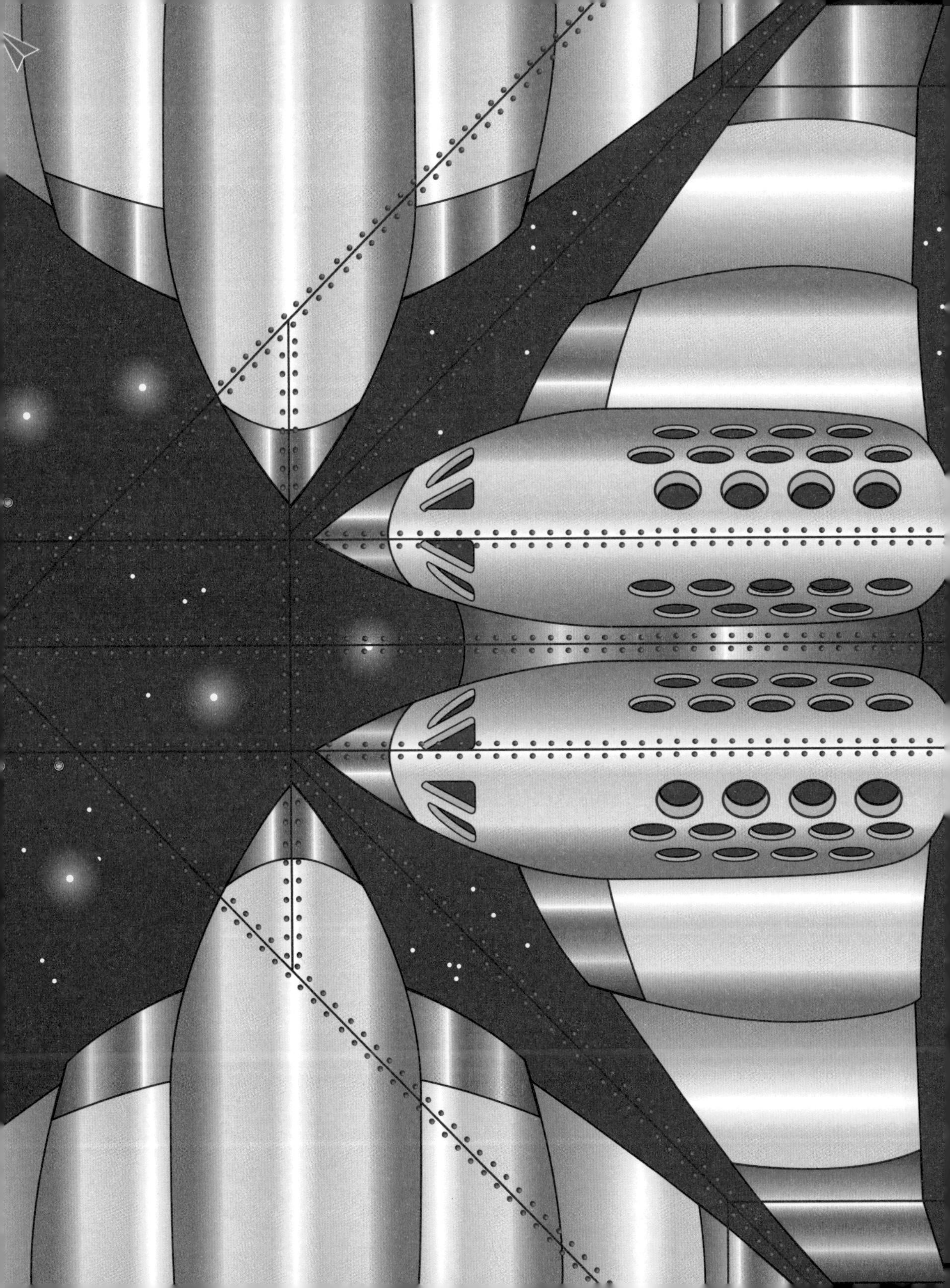

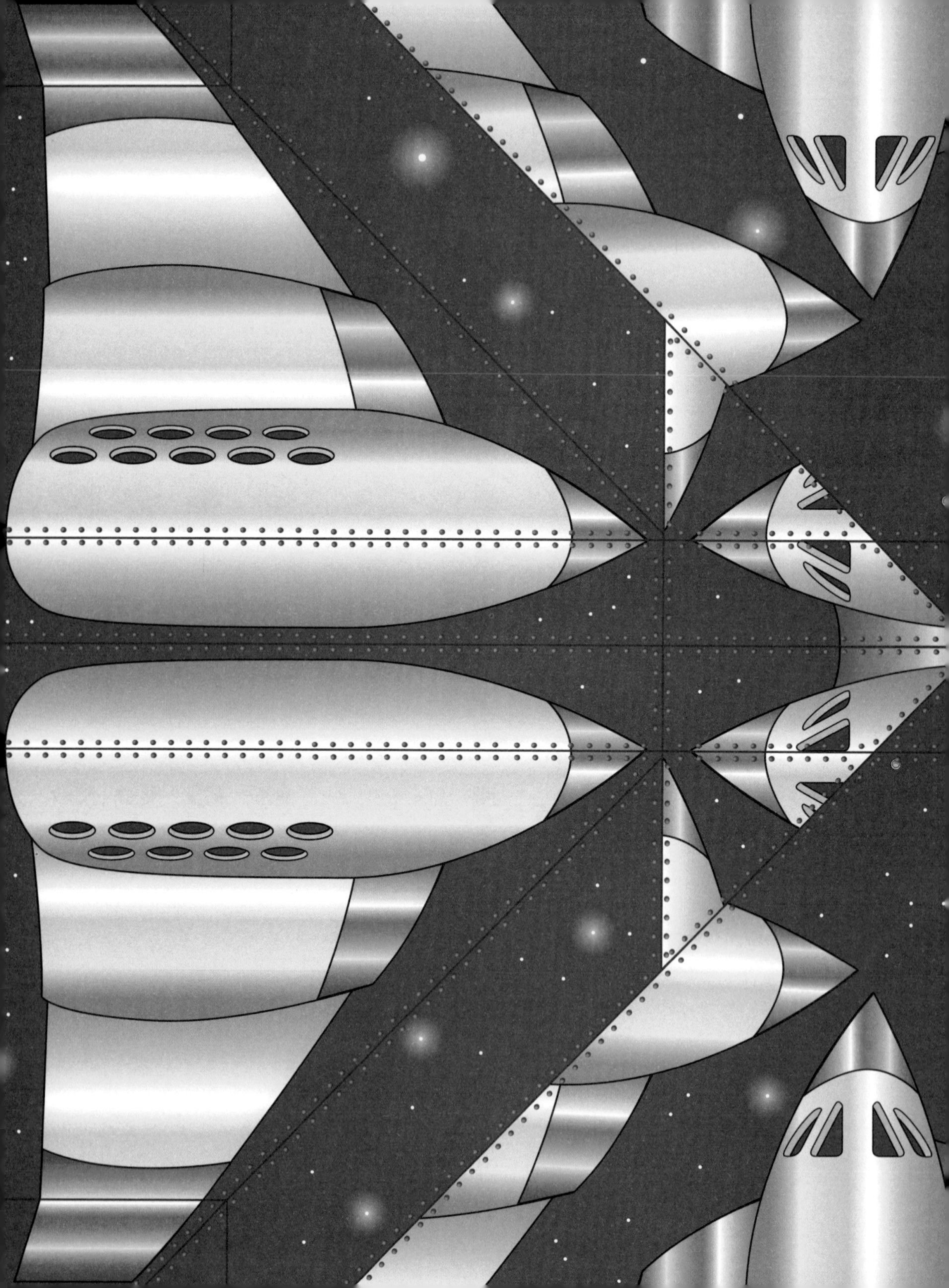

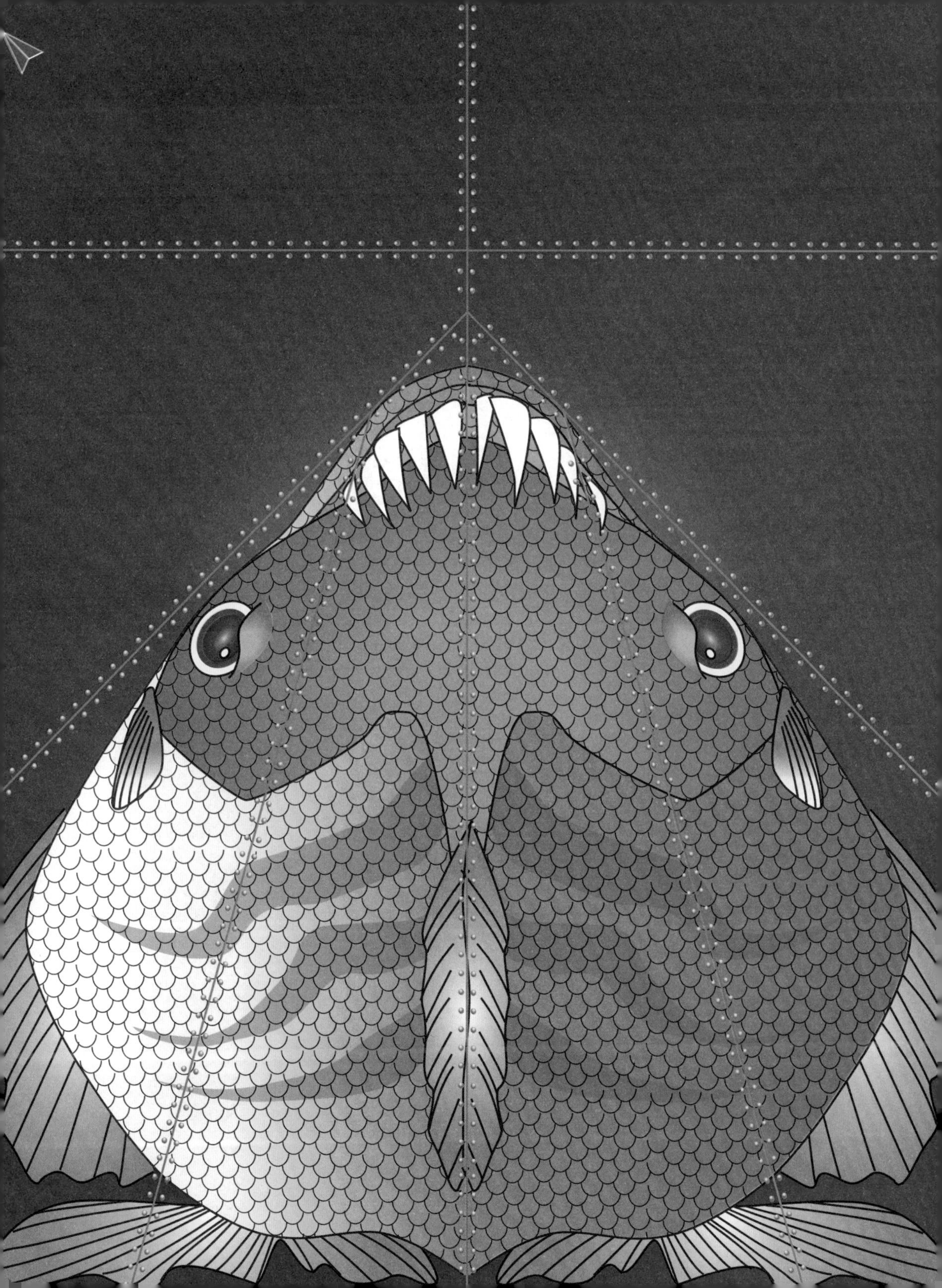

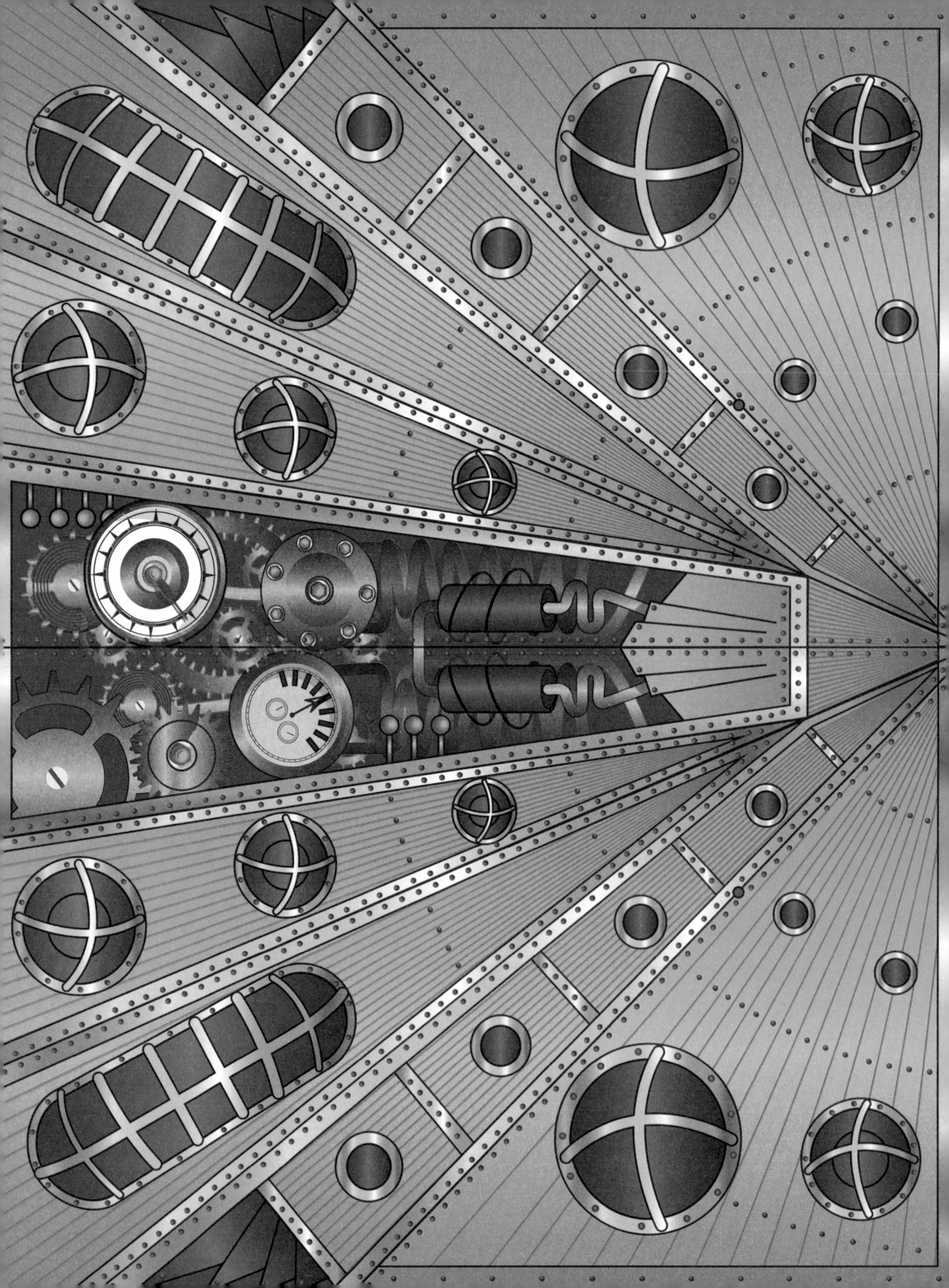

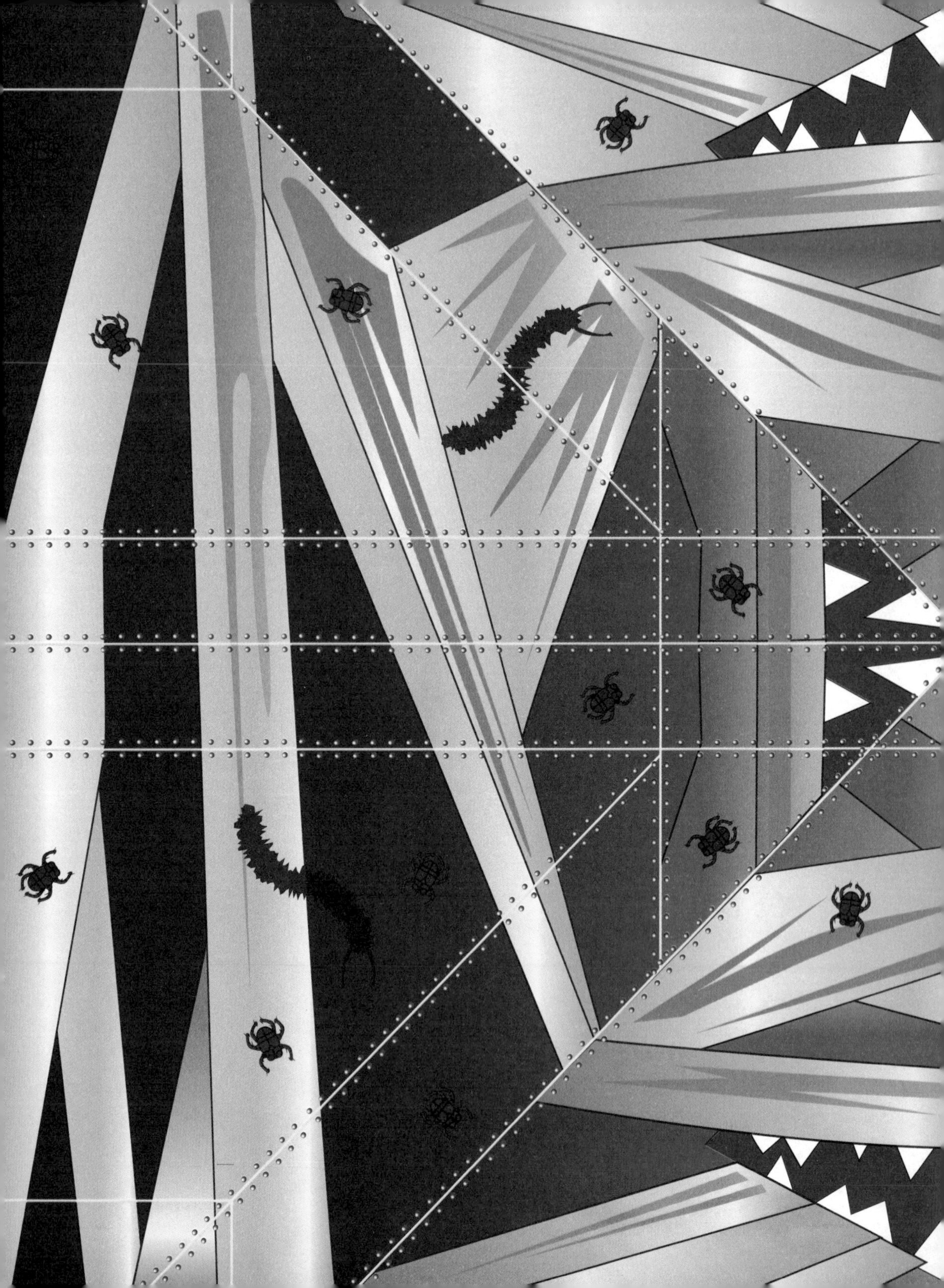

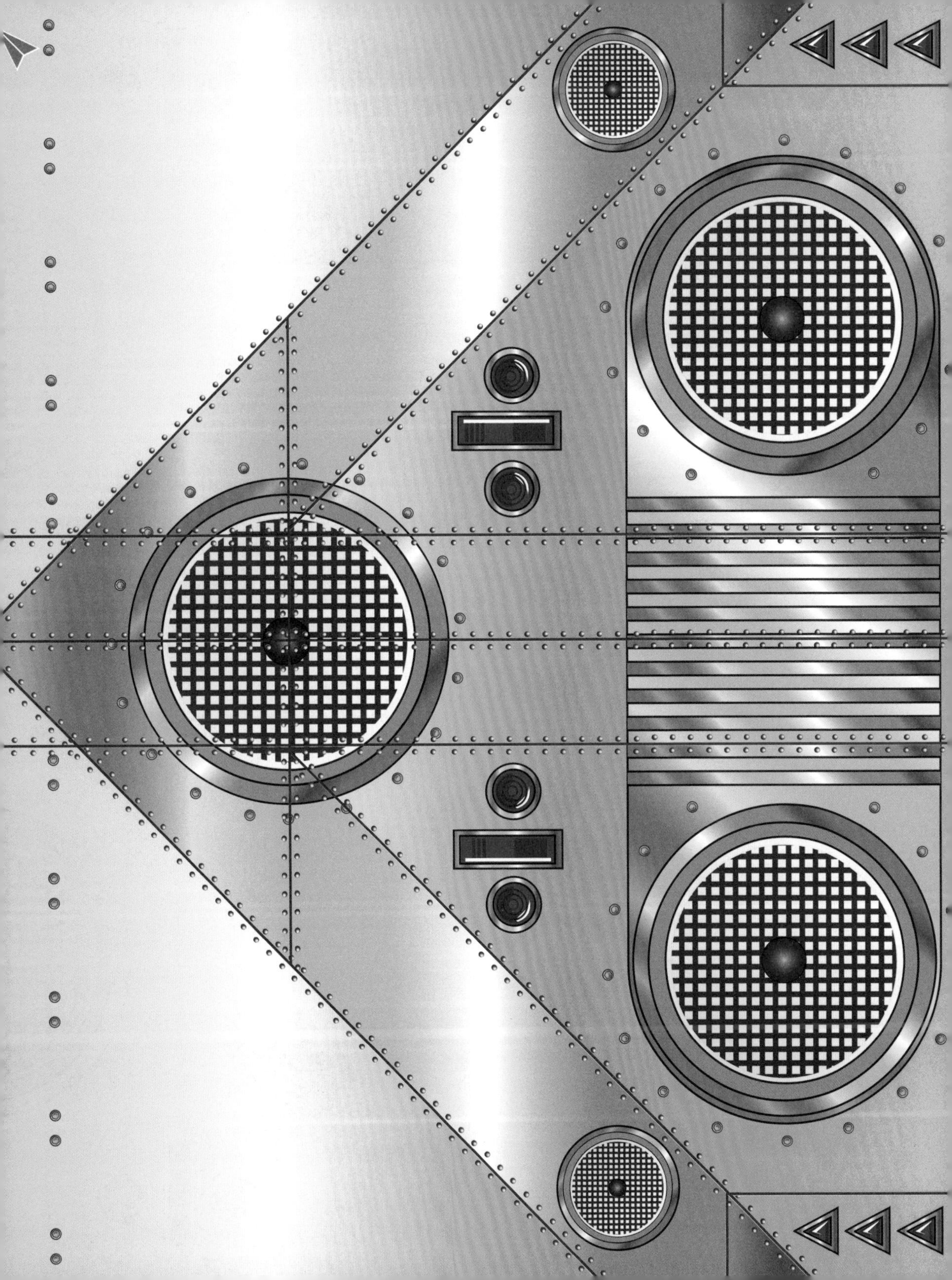

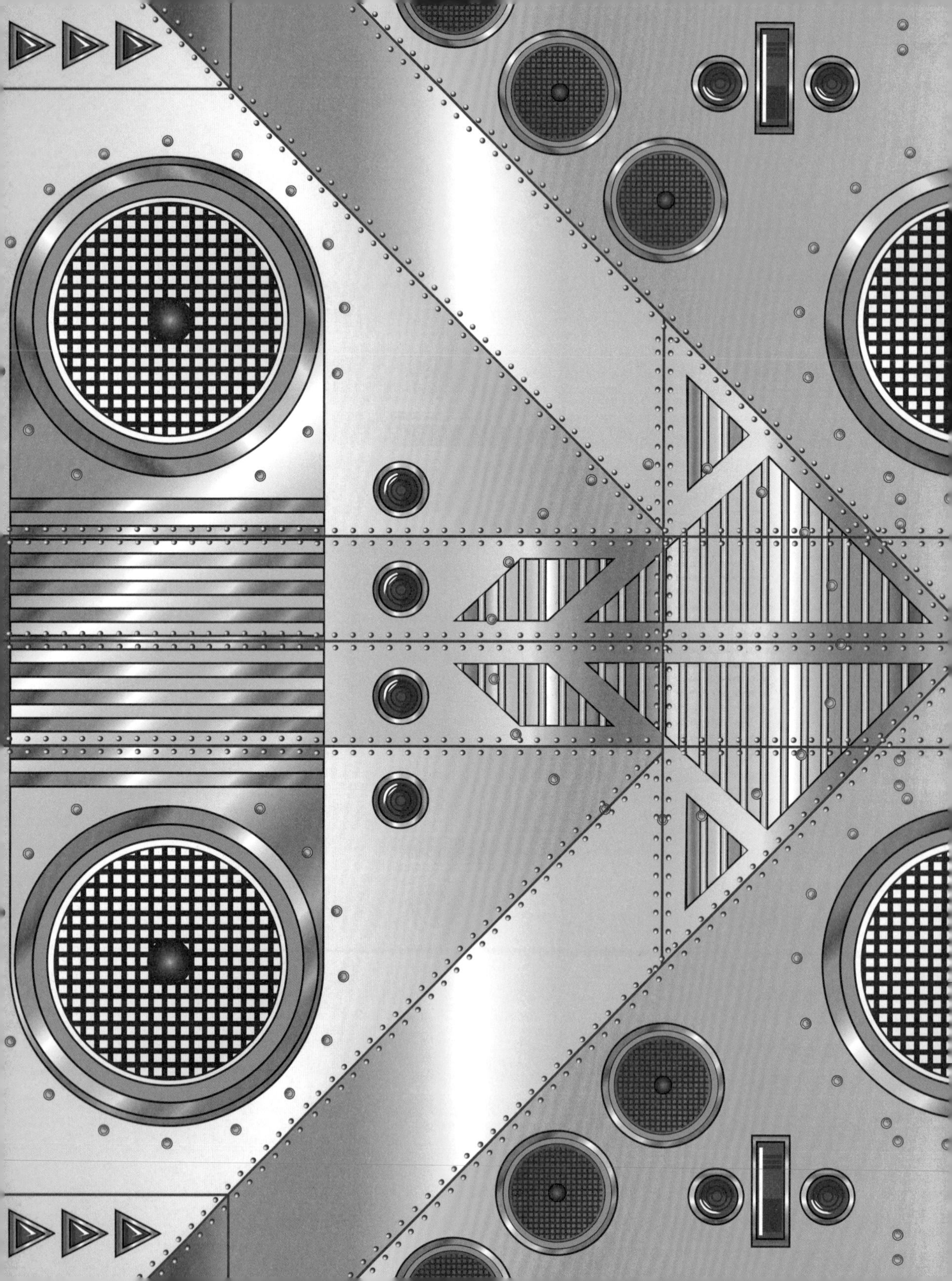

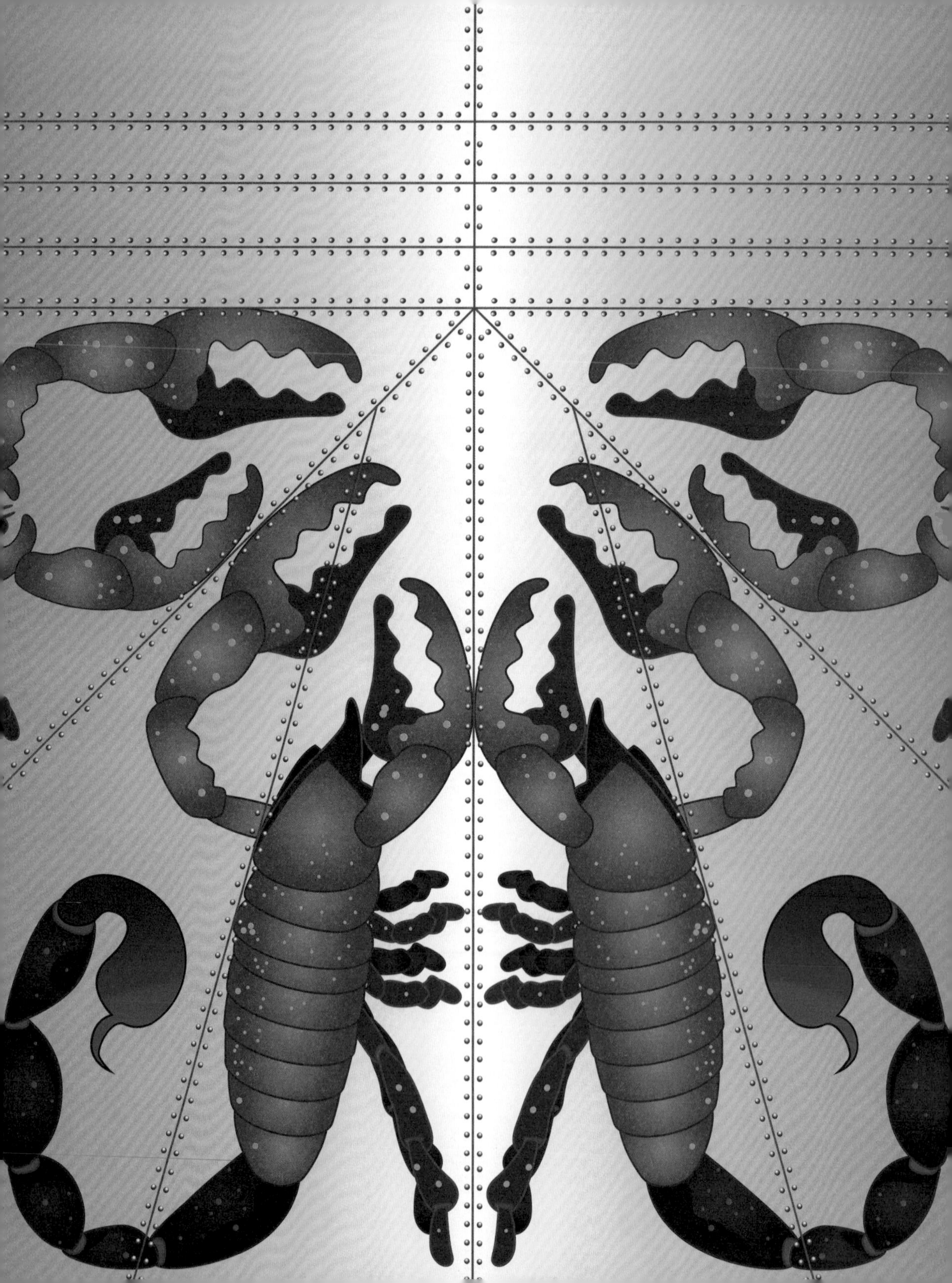

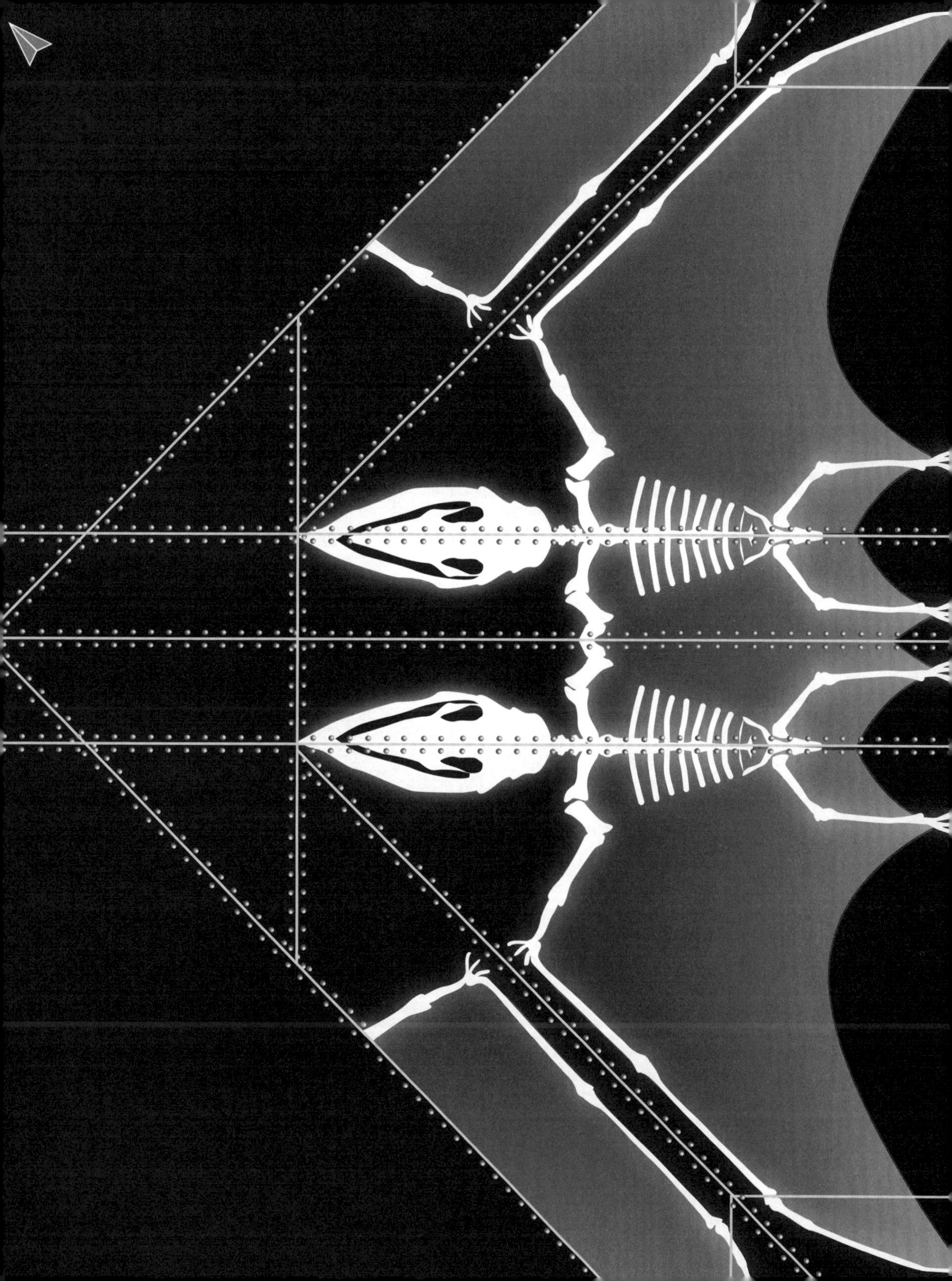

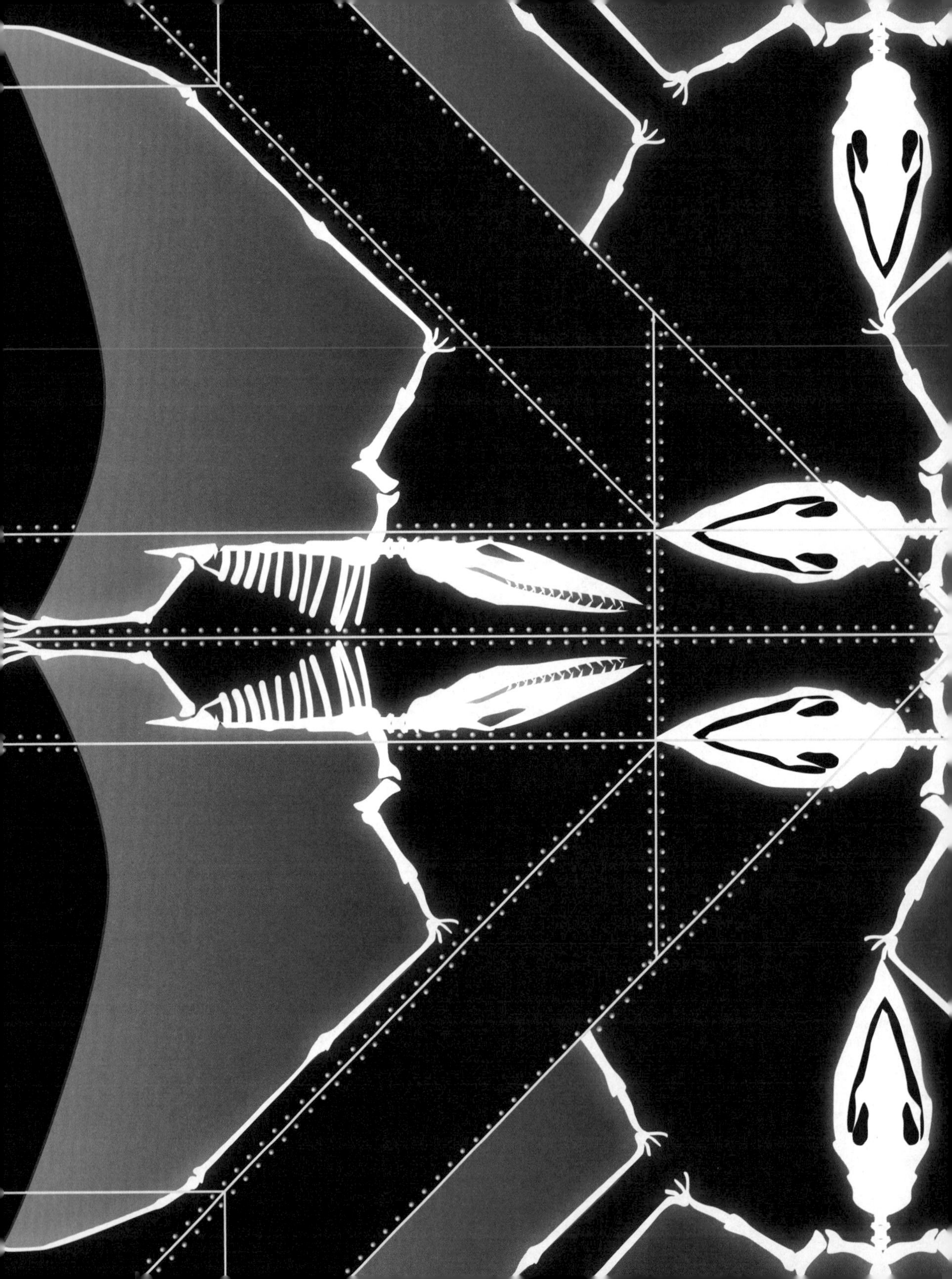

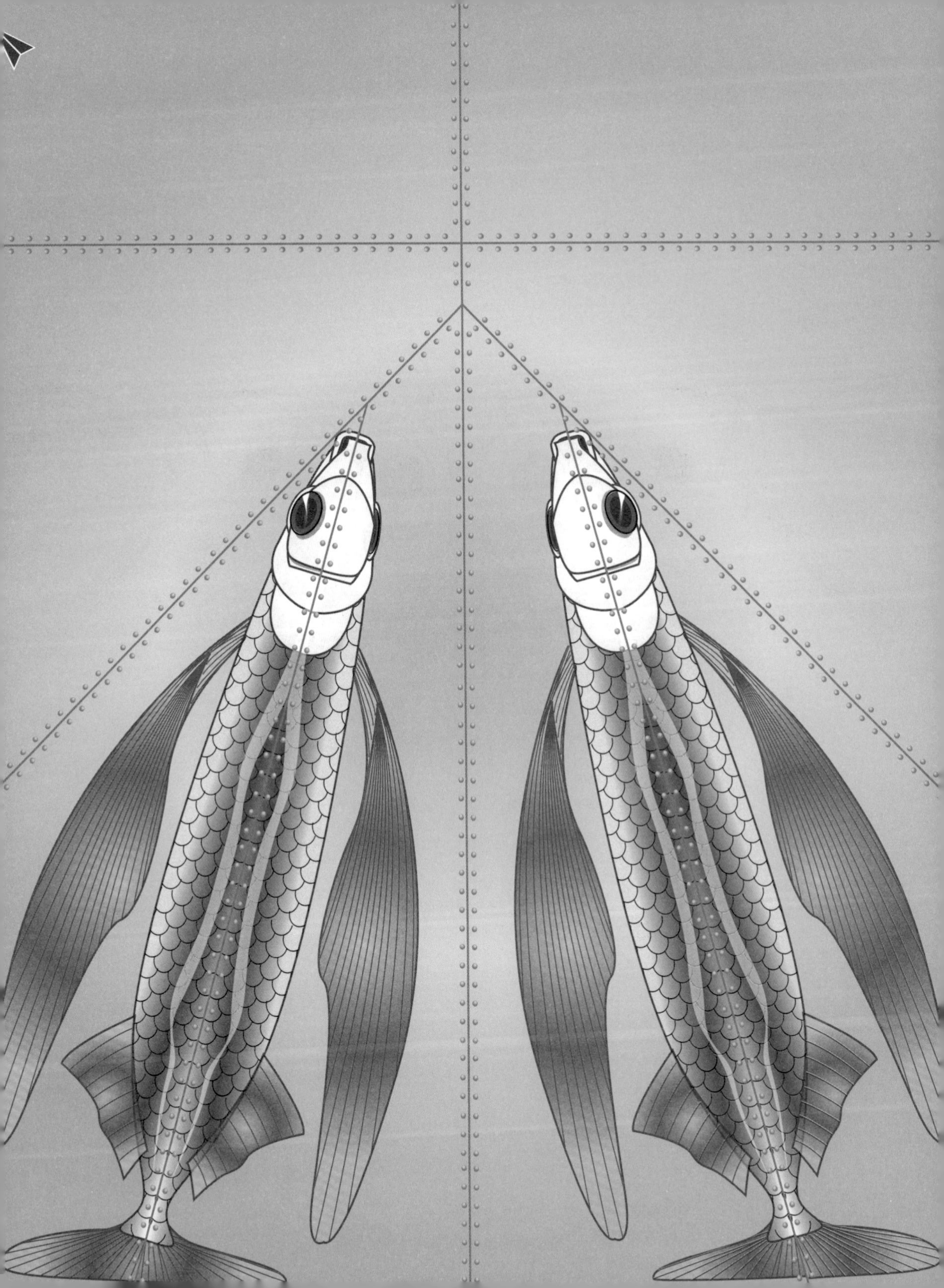

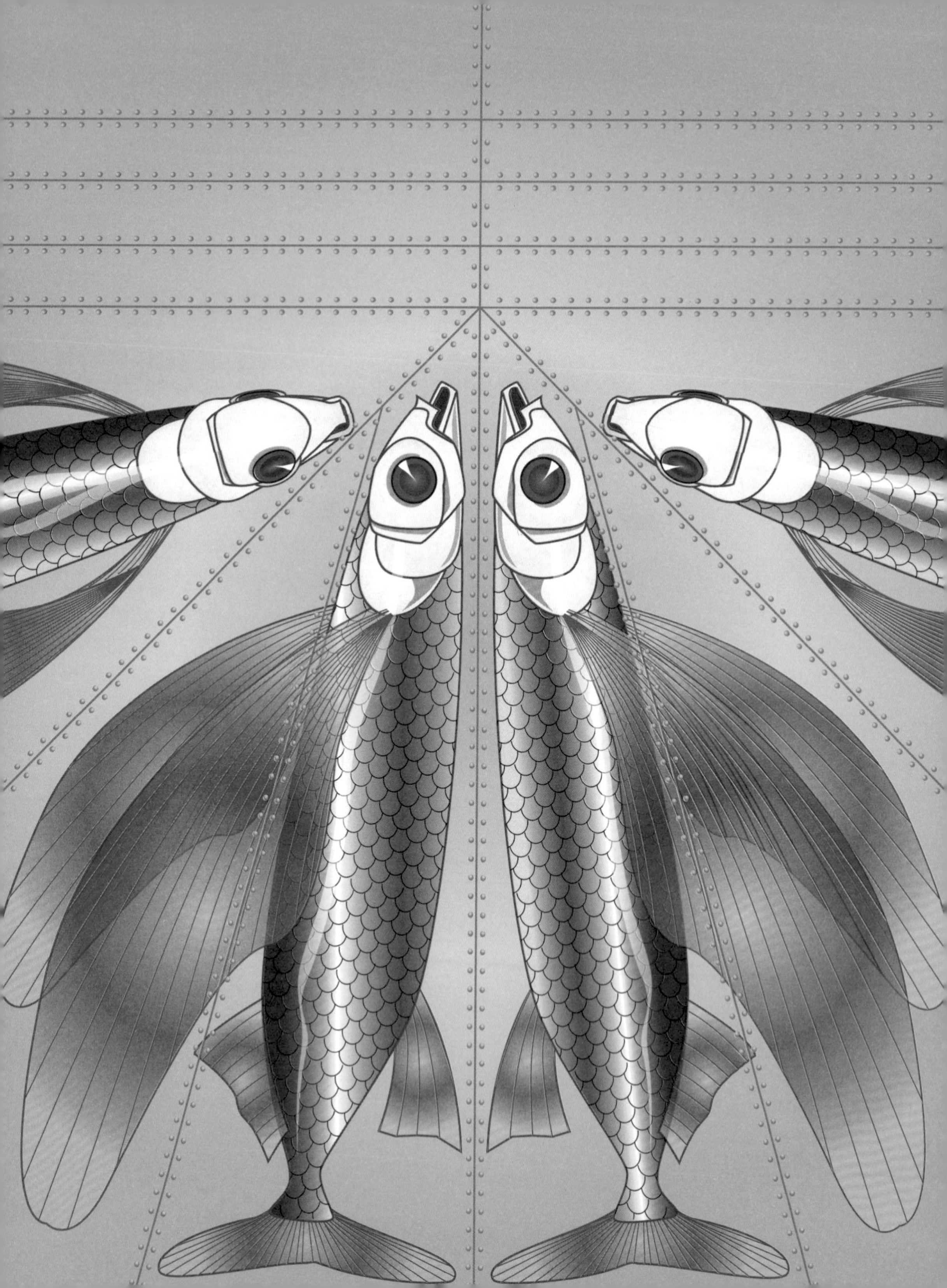

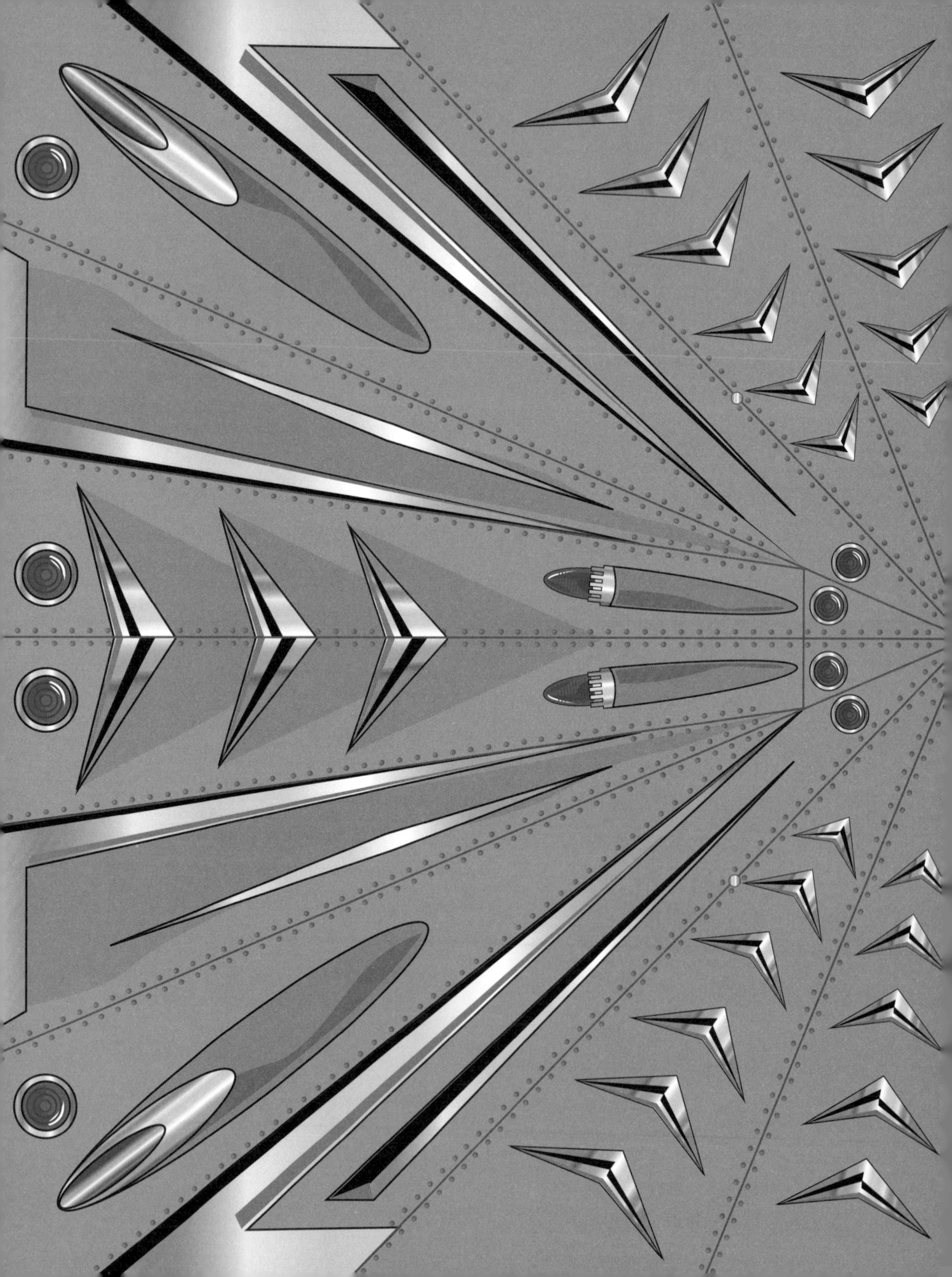

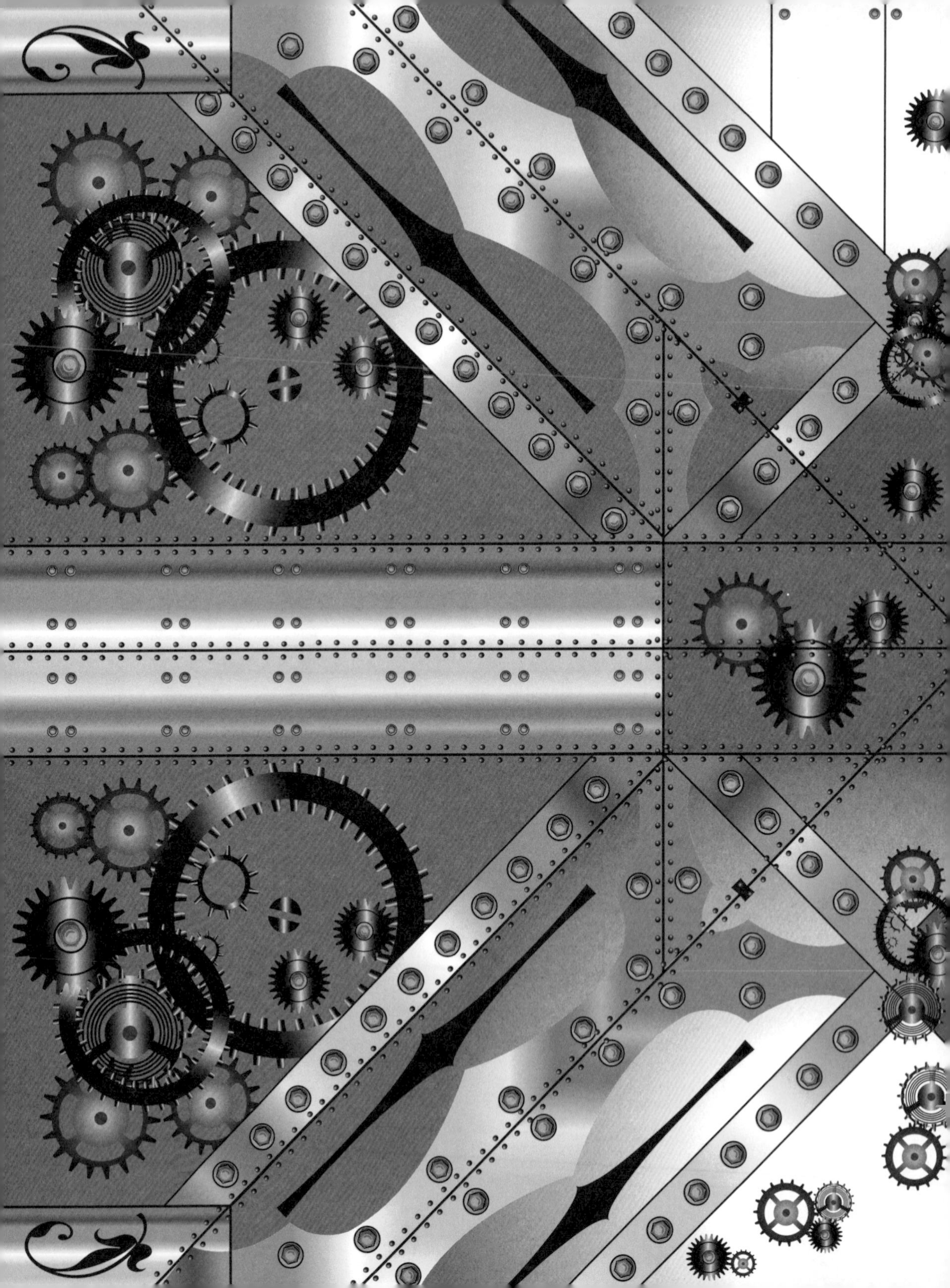

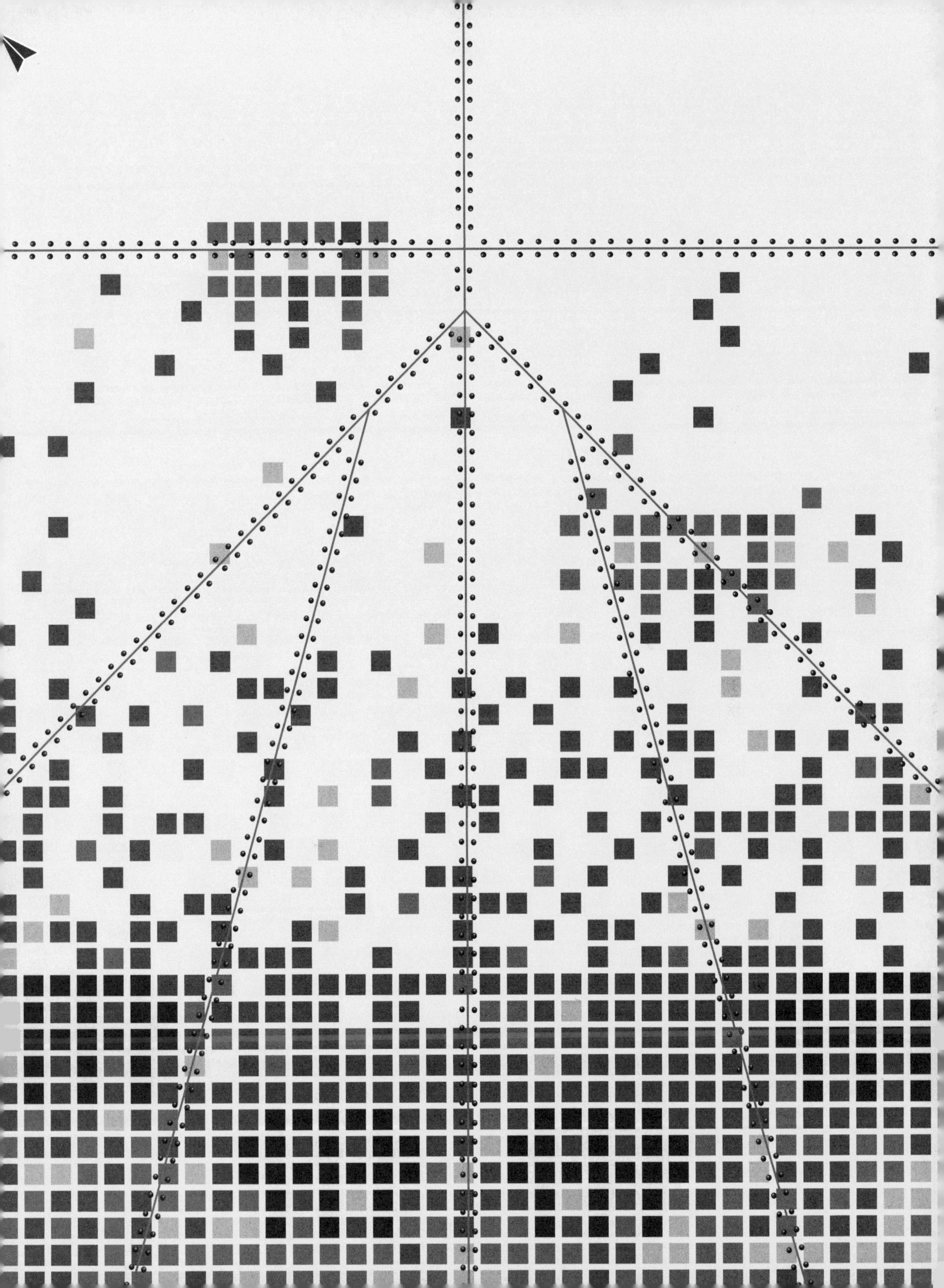

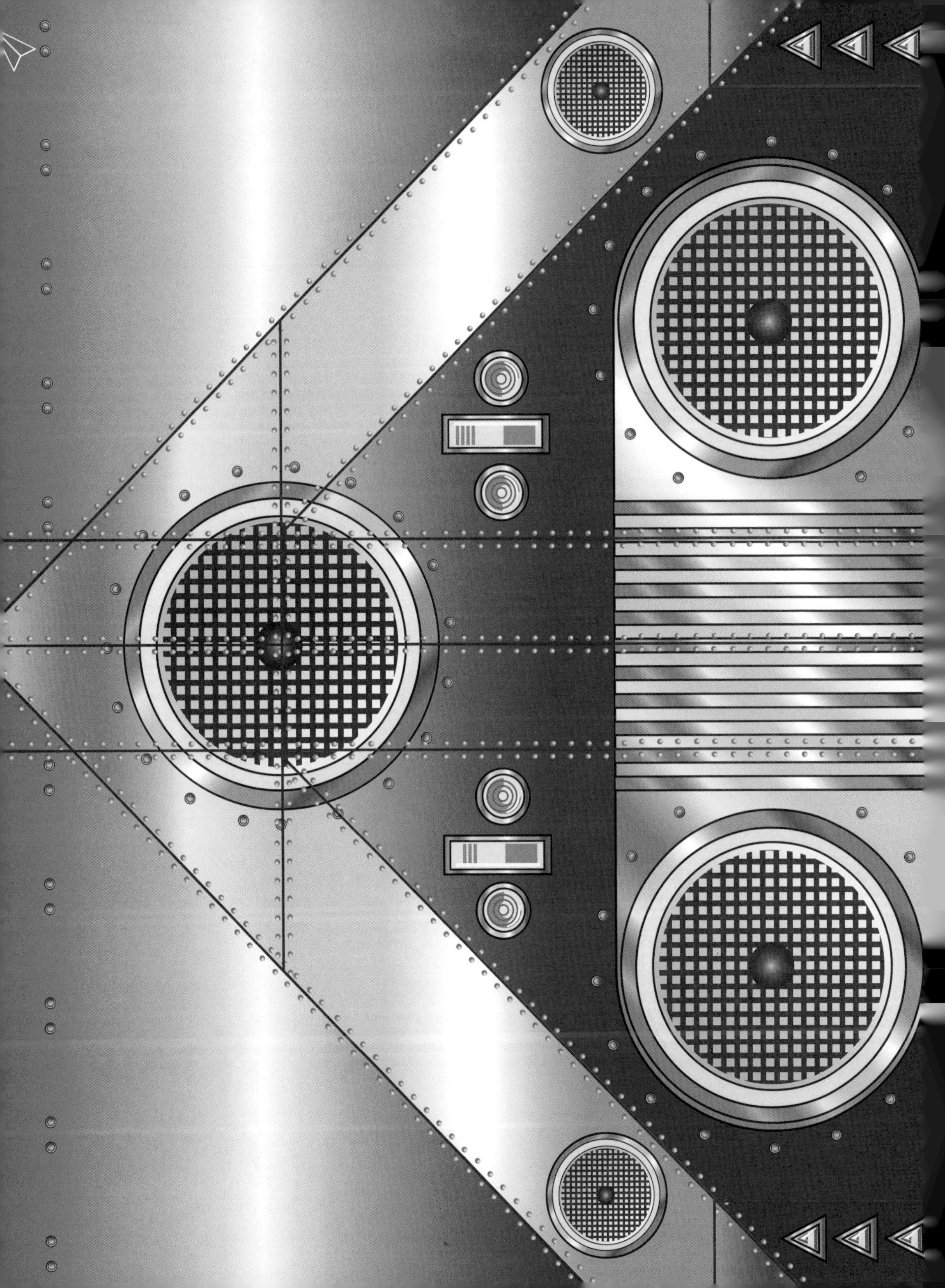

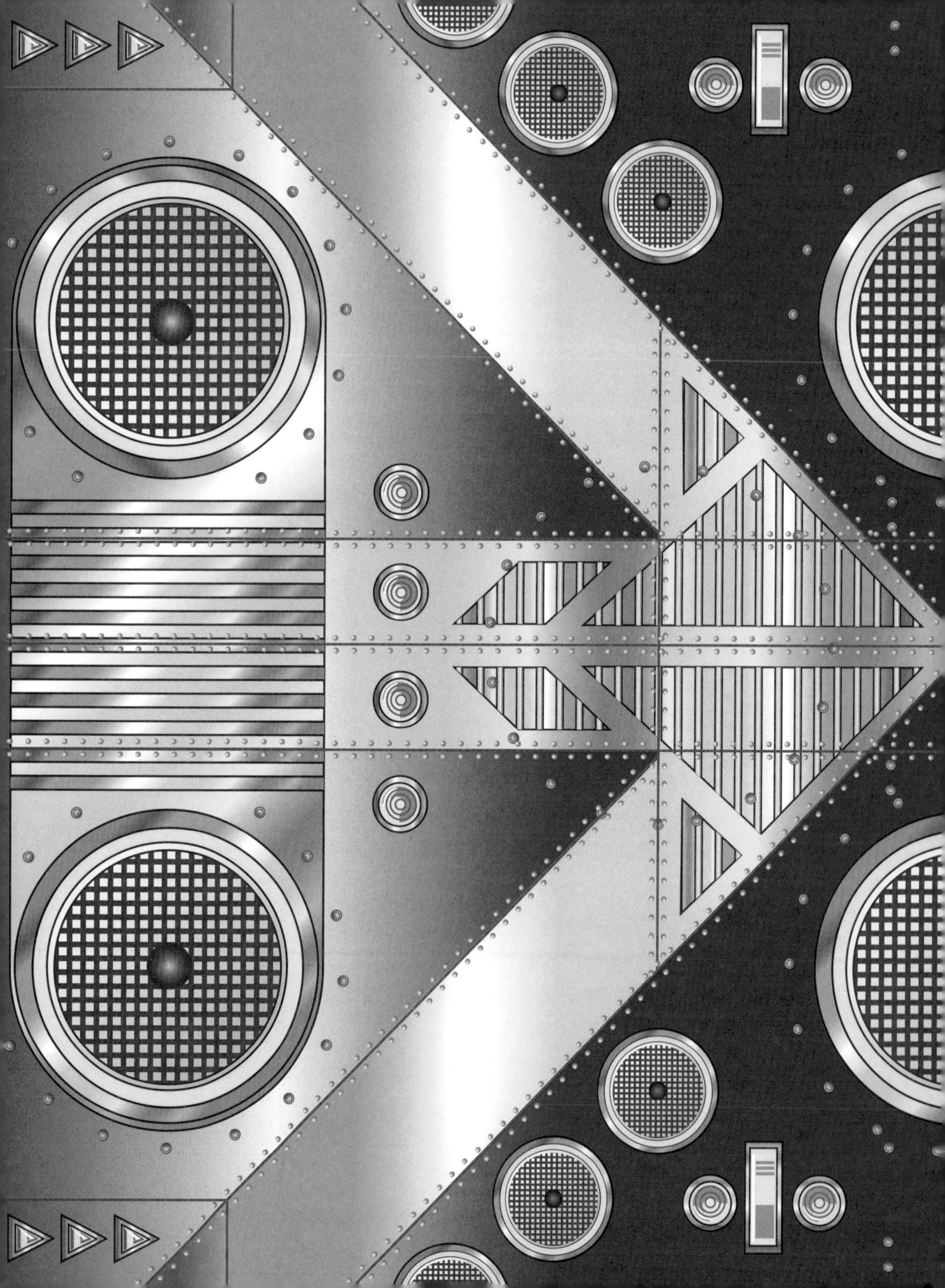

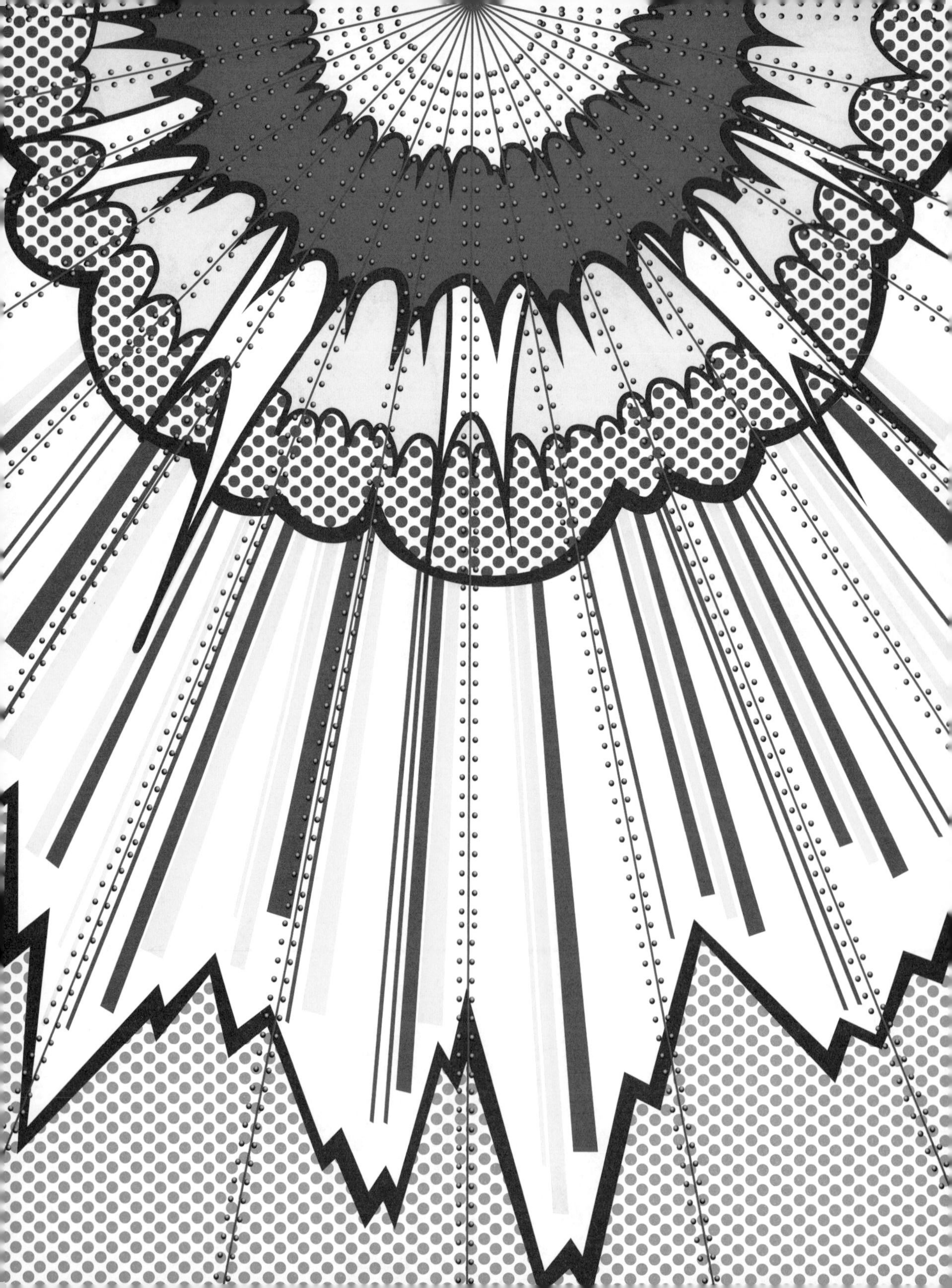

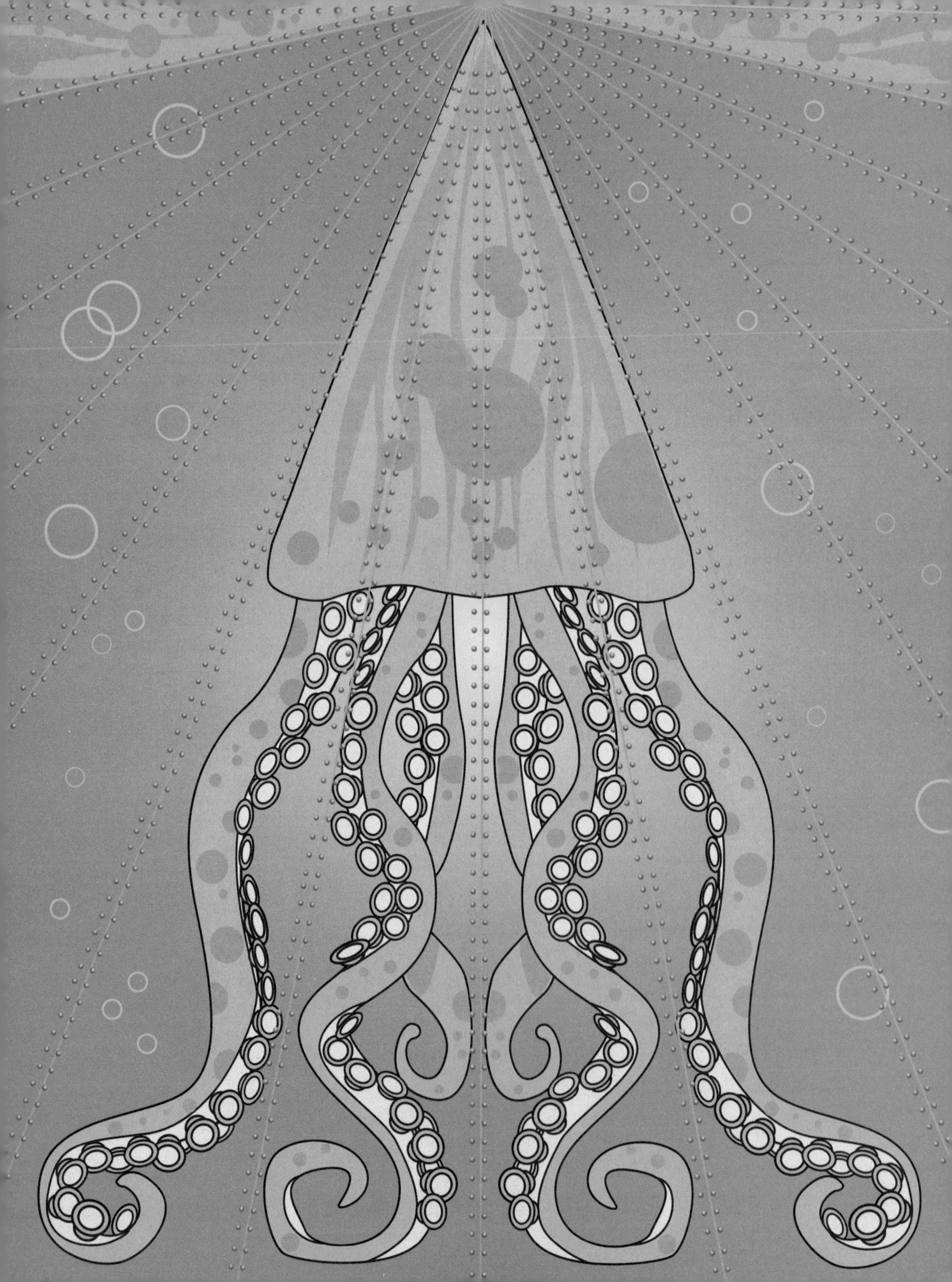

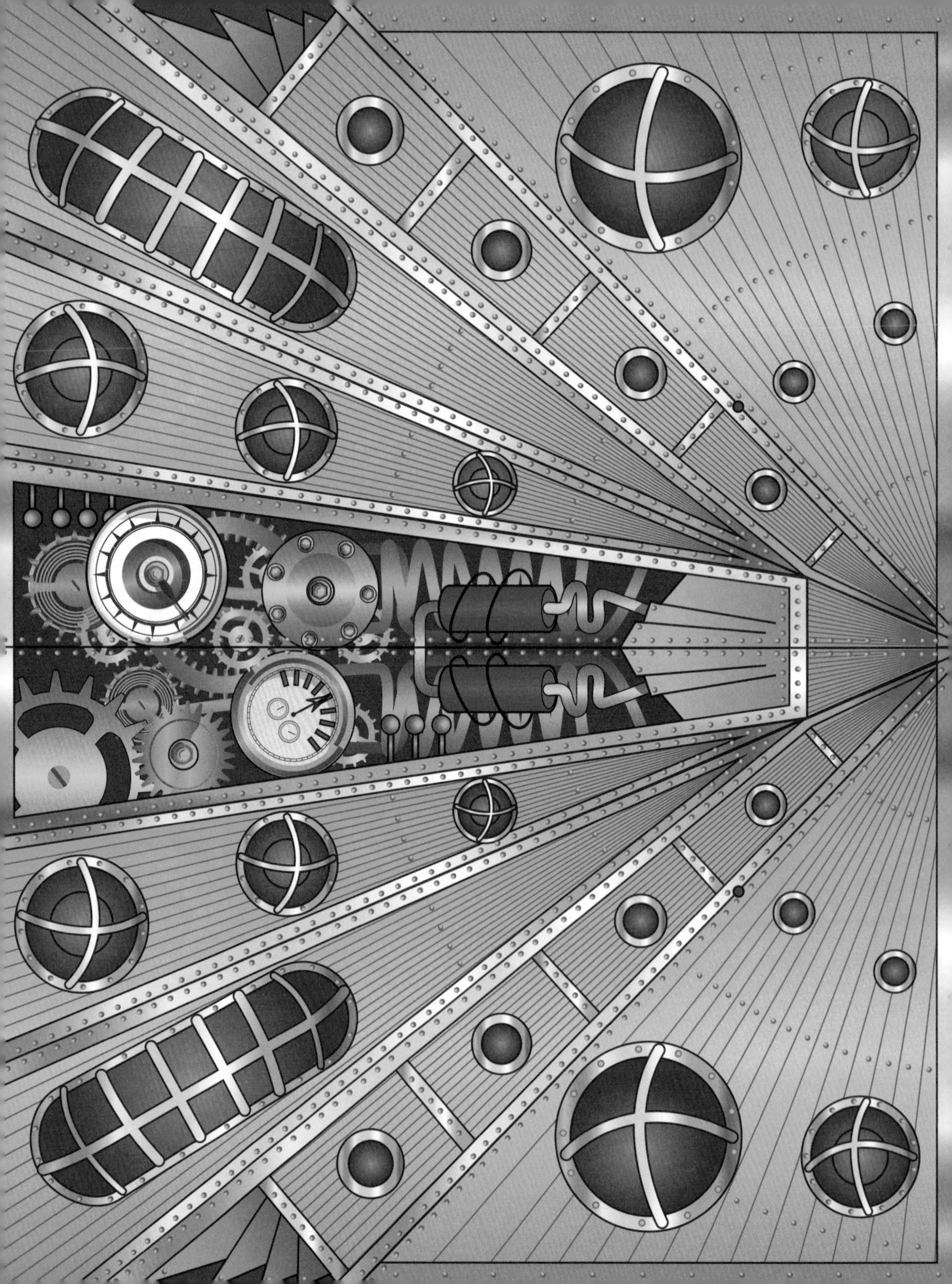

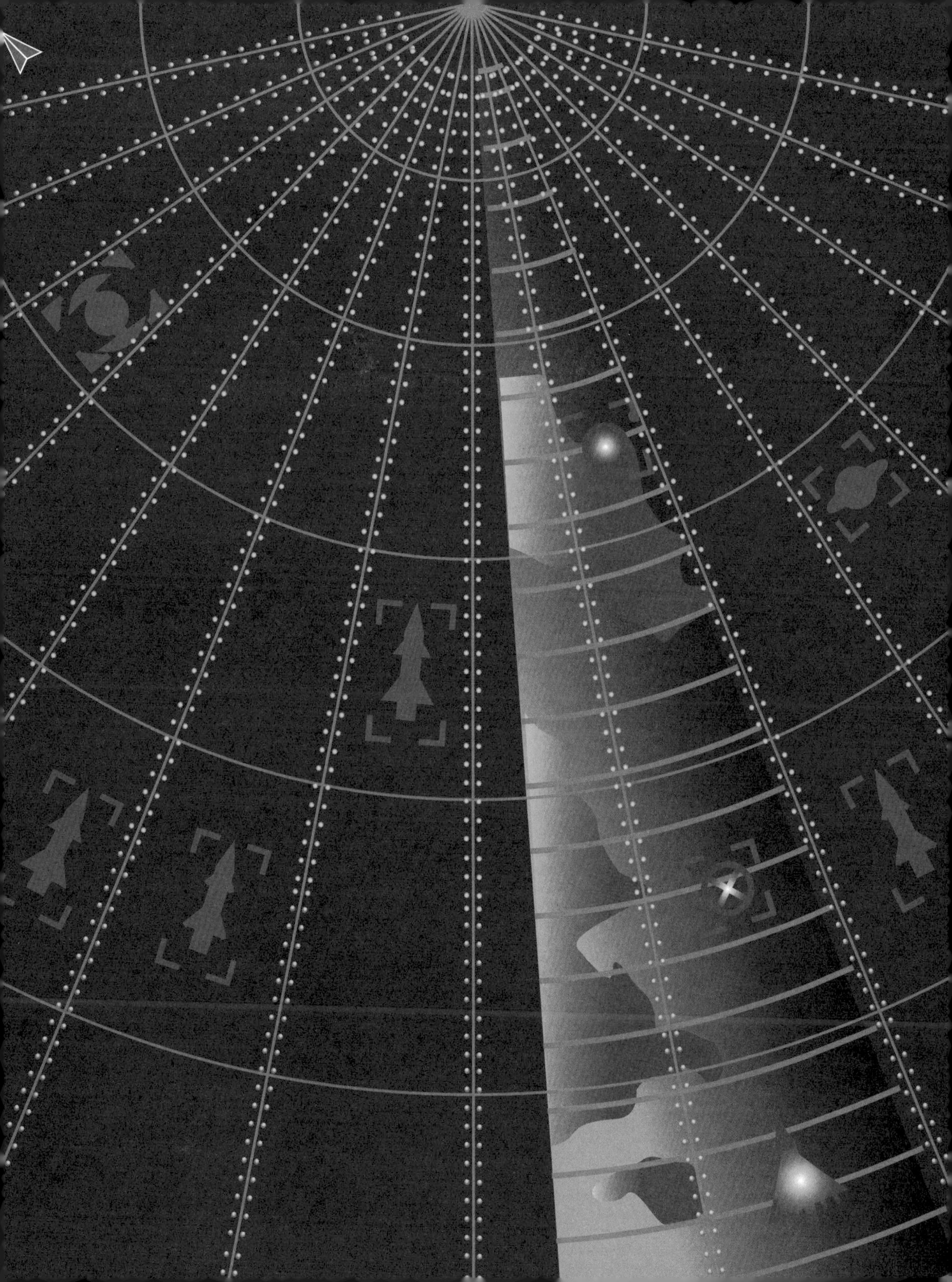

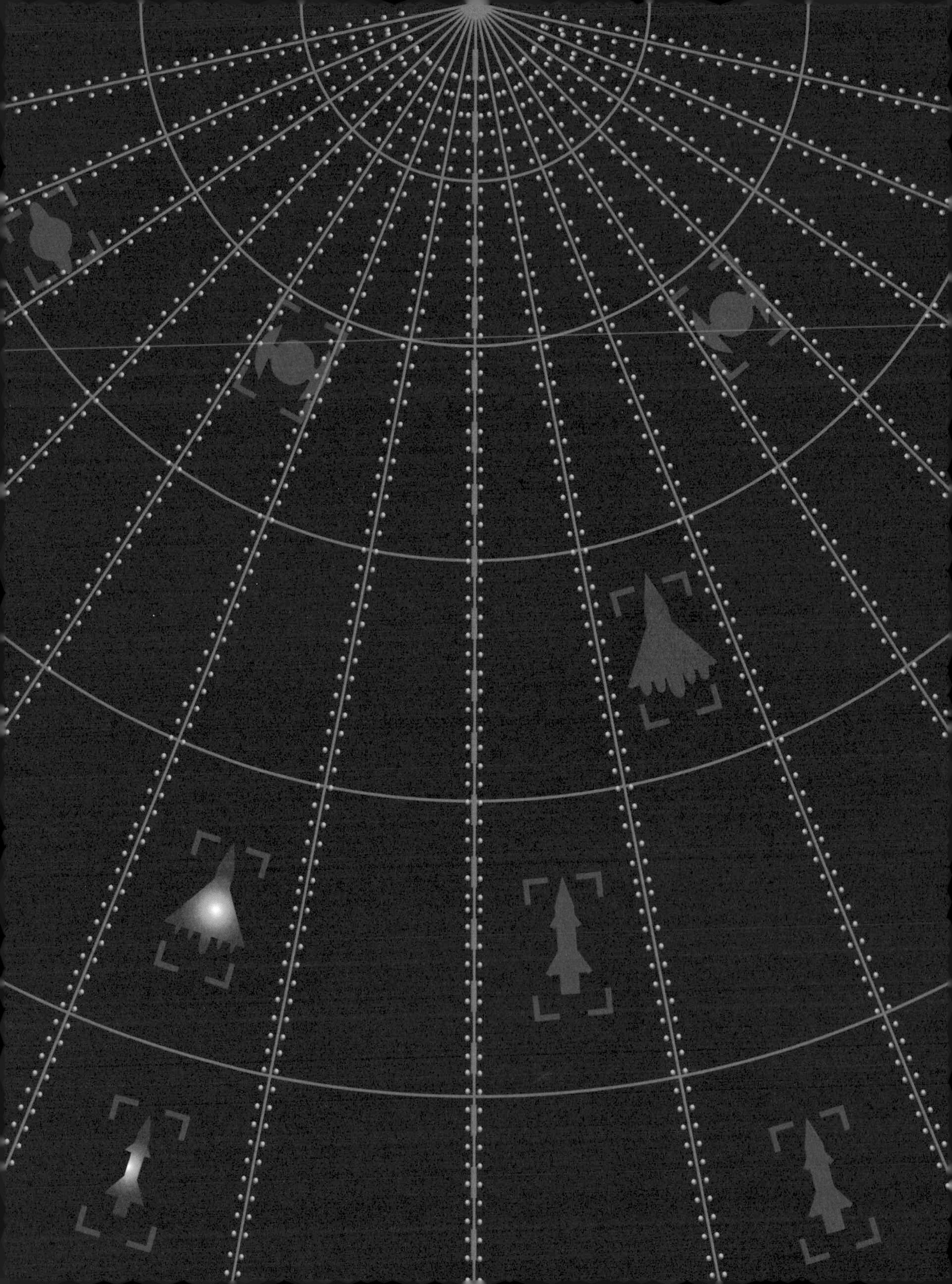

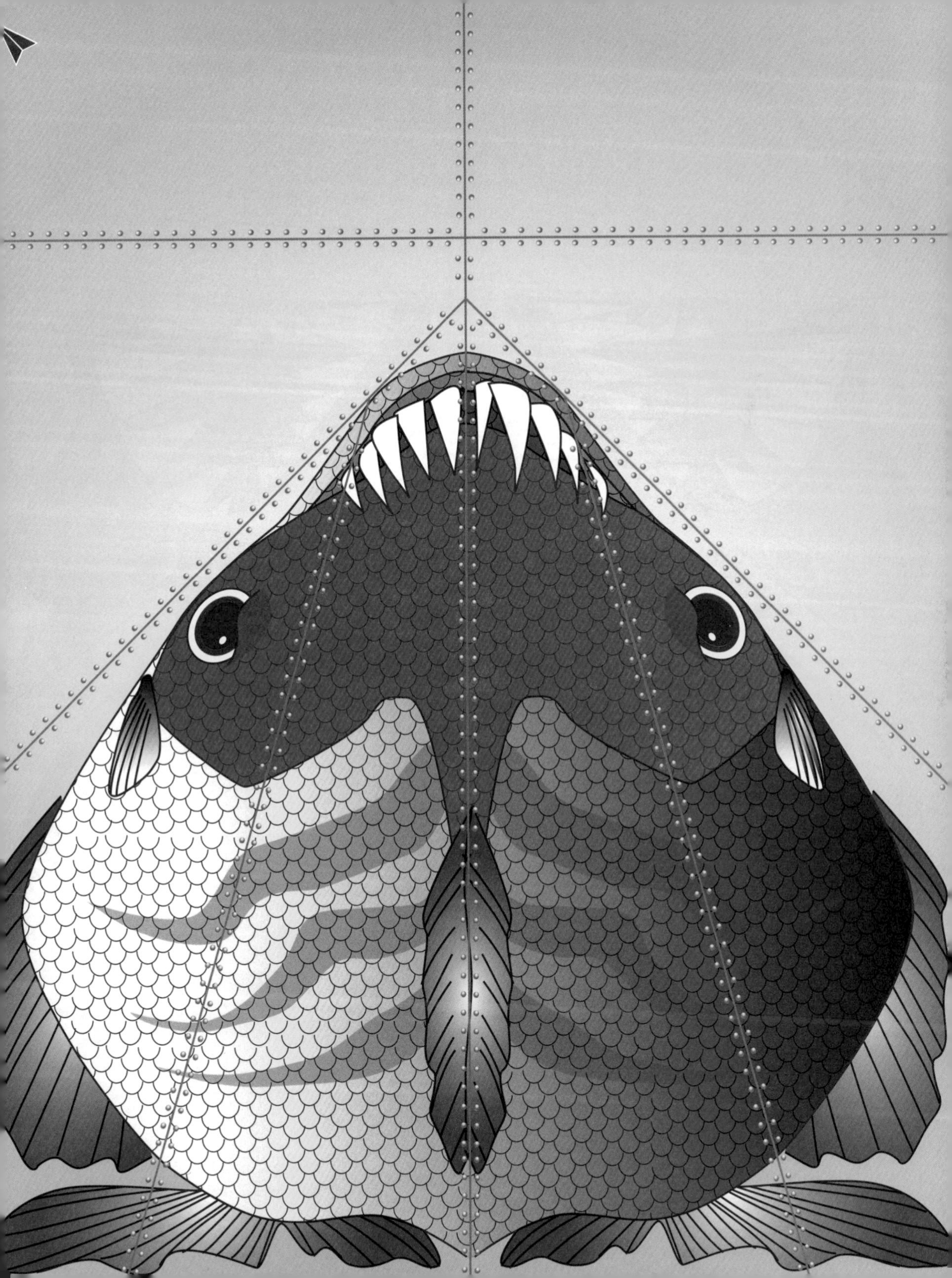

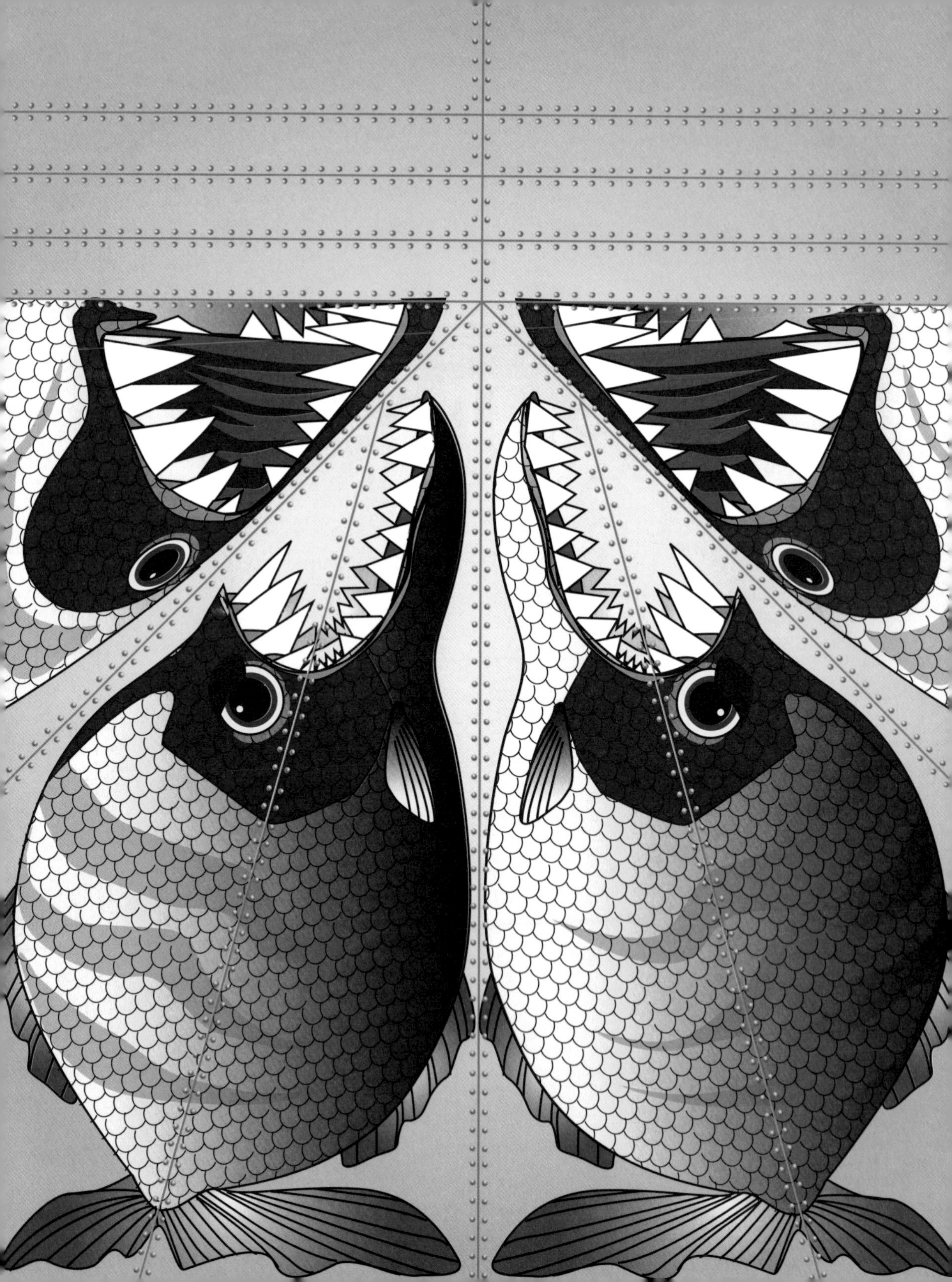

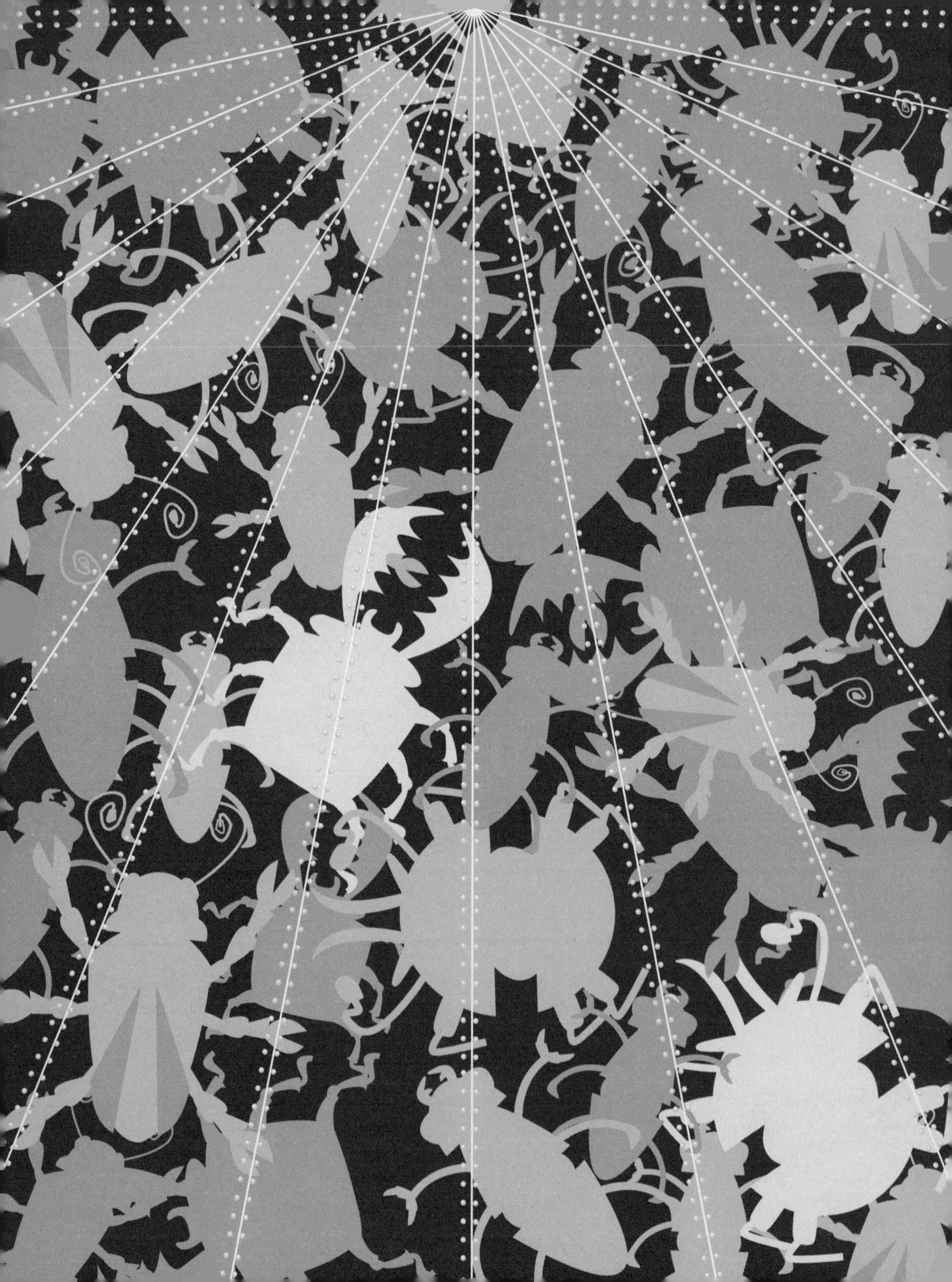

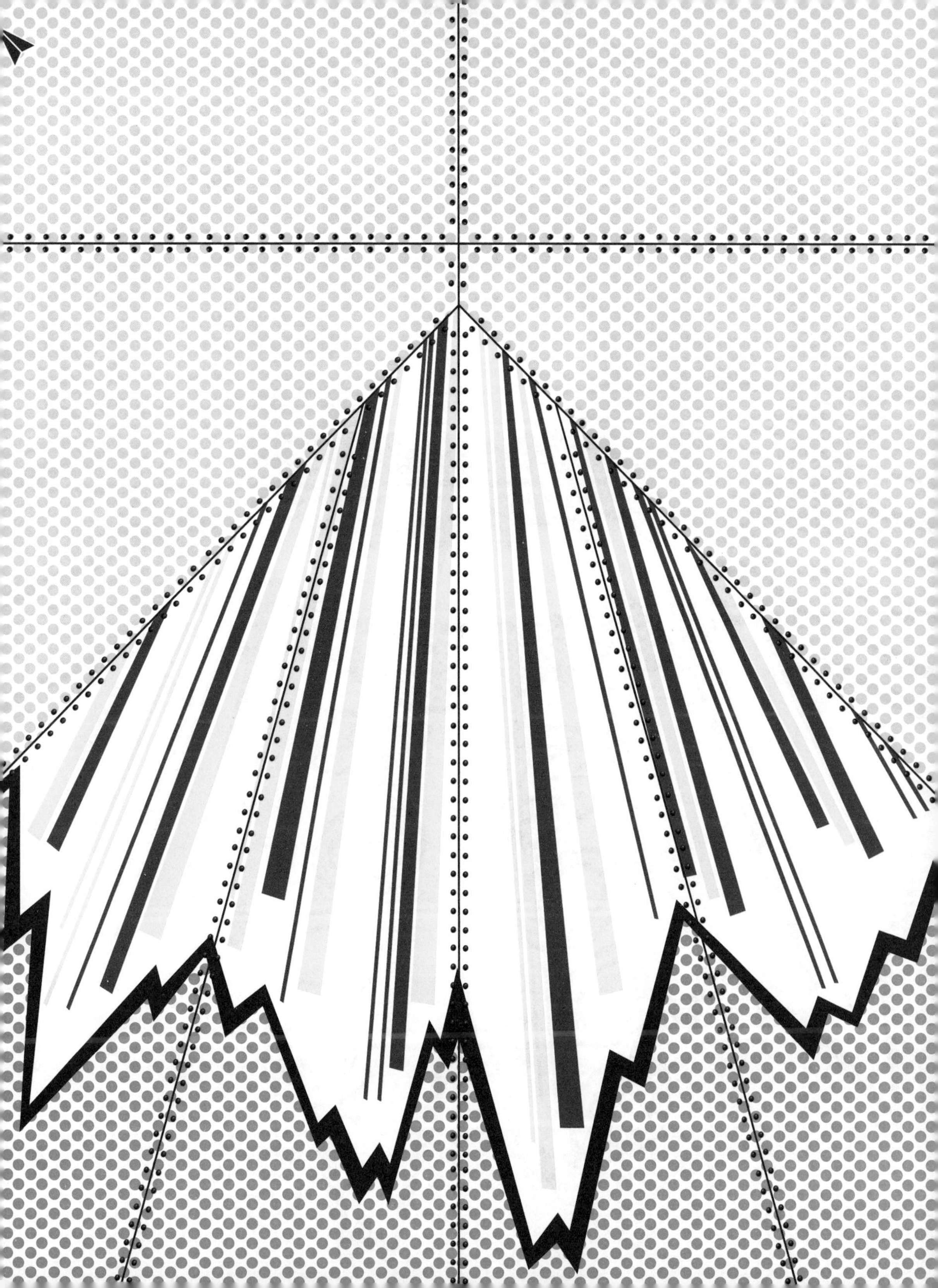

ZOOOM
ZOOOM

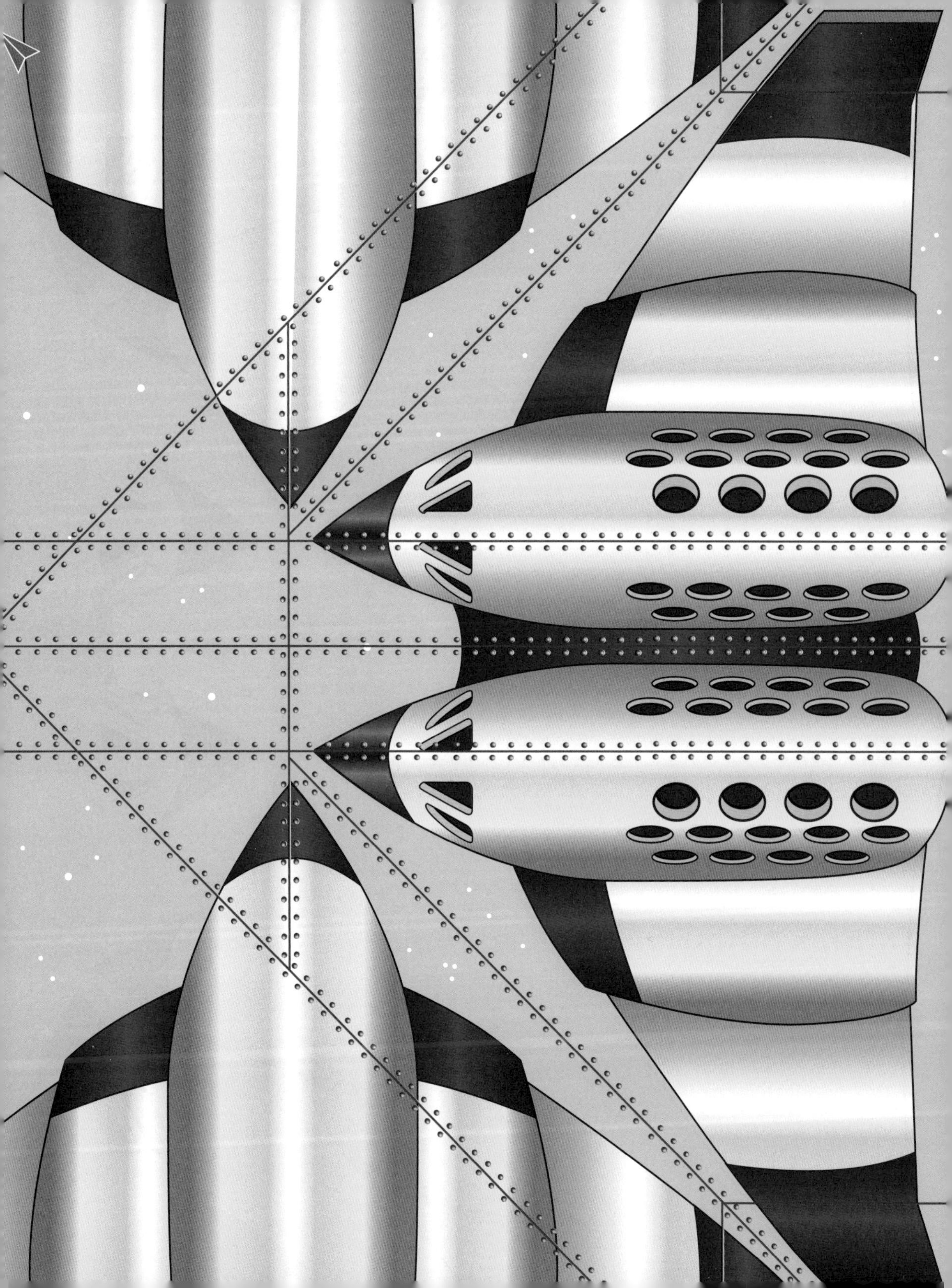

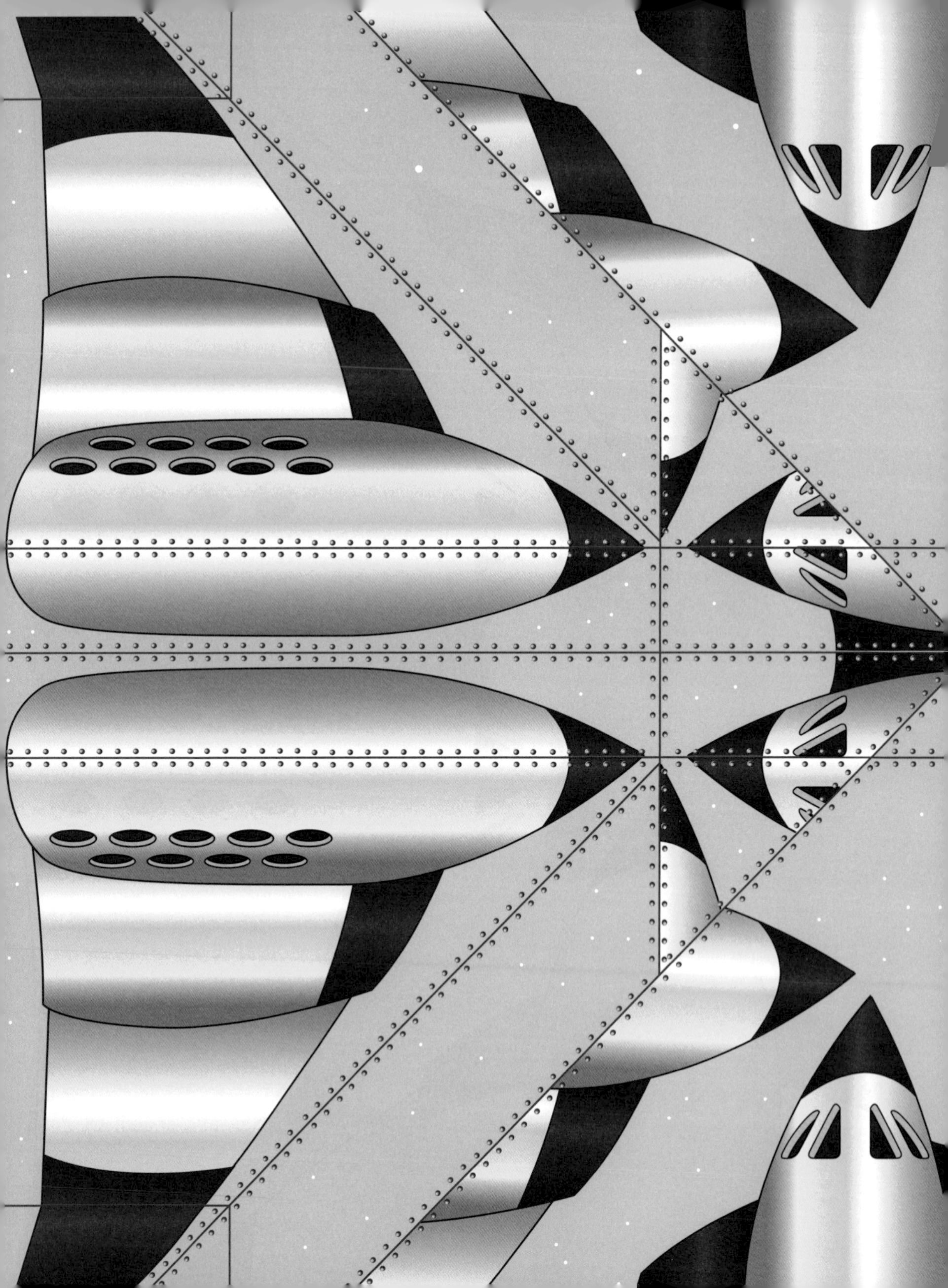

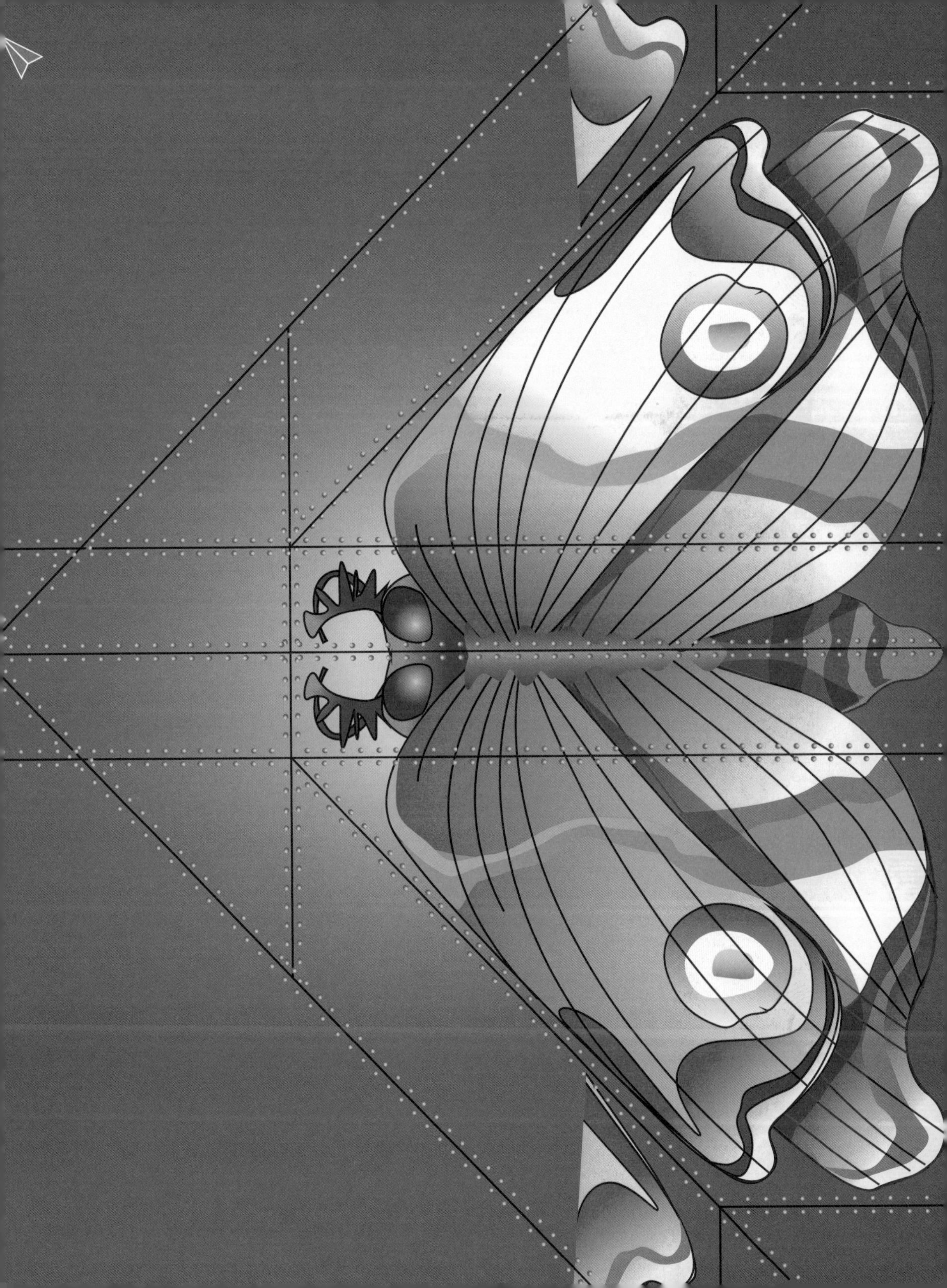

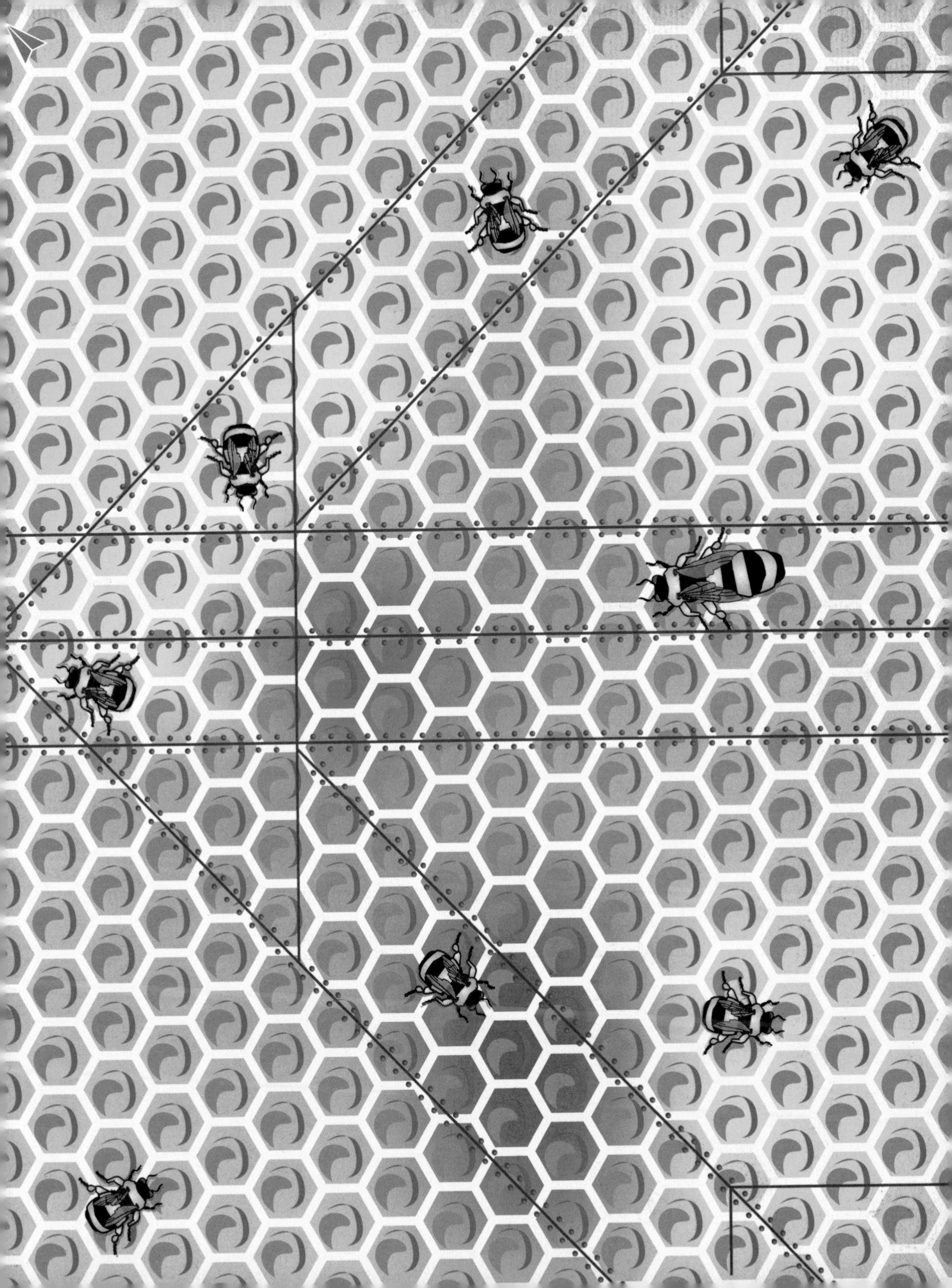

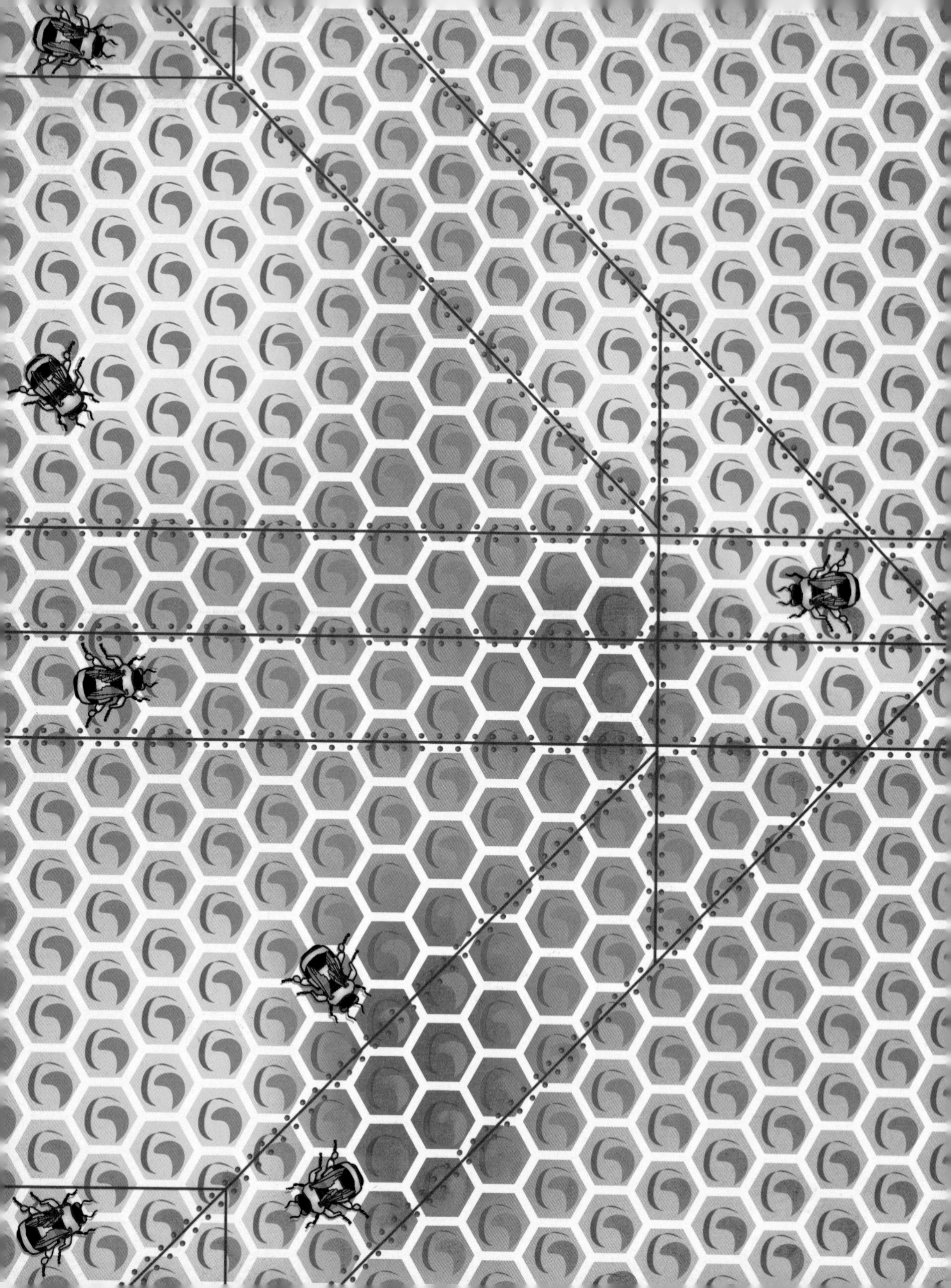

ZOOOM
ZOOOM

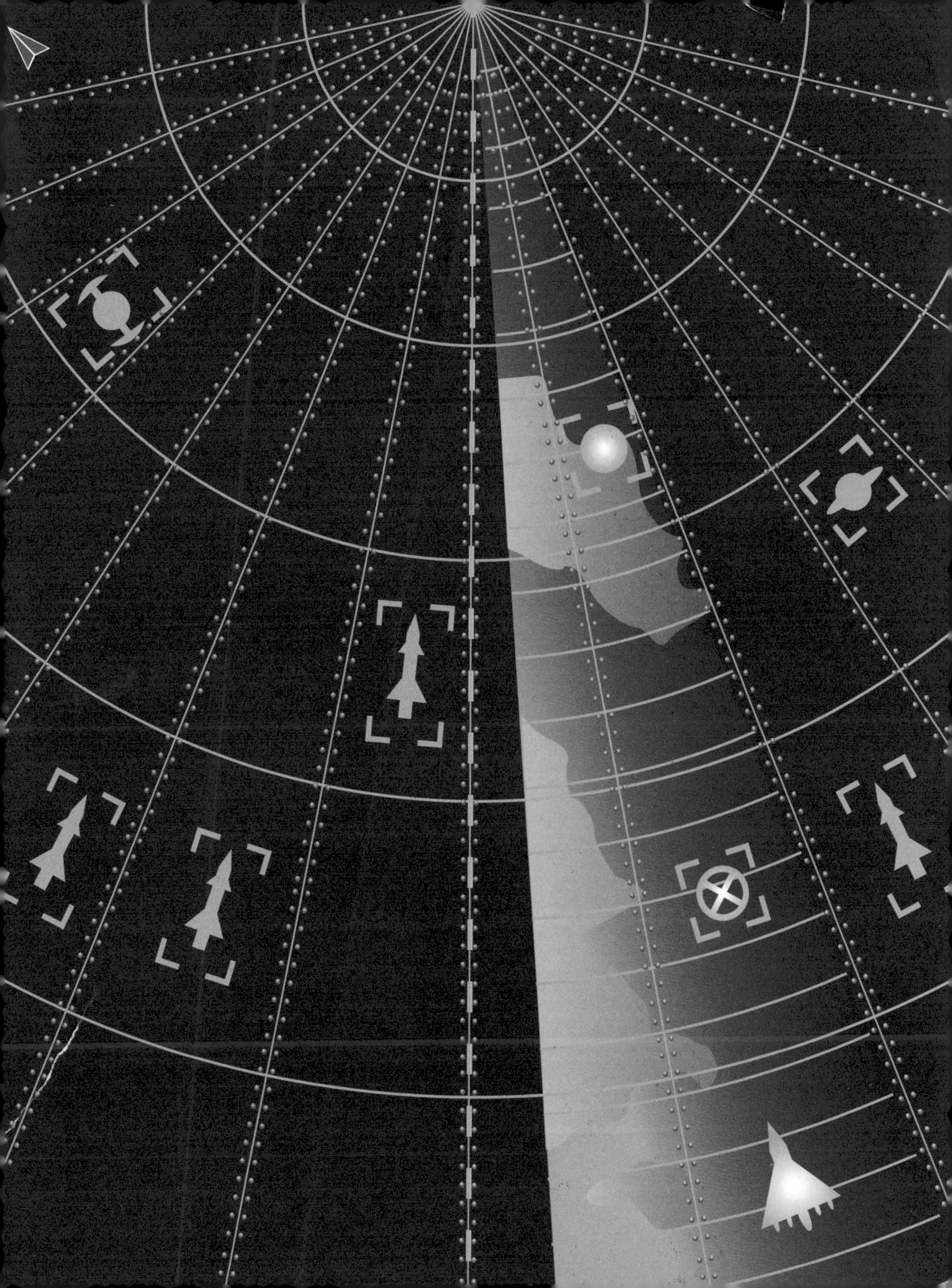